EMERGING TRENDS AND METHODS IN INTERNATIONAL SECURITY

PROCEEDINGS OF A WORKSHOP

Elizabeth Townsend, *Rapporteur*

Board on Behavioral, Cognitive, and Sensory Sciences

Division of Behavioral and Social Sciences and Education

The National Academies of
SCIENCES • ENGINEERING • MEDICINE

THE NATIONAL ACADEMIES PRESS
Washington, DC
www.nap.edu

THE NATIONAL ACADEMIES PRESS 500 Fifth Street, NW Washington, DC 20001

This activity was supported by Contract No. 10003166 between the National Academy of Sciences and the Office of the Director of National Intelligence, Any opinions, findings, conclusions, or recommendations expressed in this publication do not necessarily reflect the views of any organization or agency that provided support for the project.

International Standard Book Number-13: 978-0-309-47387-3
International Standard Book Number-10: 0-309-47387-X
Digital Object Identifier: https://doi.org/10.17226/25058

Additional copies of this publication are available for sale from the National Academies Press, 500 Fifth Street, NW, Keck 360, Washington, DC 20001; (800) 624-6242 or (202) 334-3313; http://www.nap.edu.

Copyright 2018 by the National Academy of Sciences. All rights reserved.

Printed in the United States of America

Suggested citation: National Academies of Sciences, Engineering, and Medicine. (2018). *Emerging Trends and Methods in International Security: Proceedings of a Workshop*. Washington, DC: The National Academies Press. doi: https://doi.org/10.17226/25058.

The National Academies of
SCIENCES · ENGINEERING · MEDICINE

The **National Academy of Sciences** was established in 1863 by an Act of Congress, signed by President Lincoln, as a private, nongovernmental institution to advise the nation on issues related to science and technology. Members are elected by their peers for outstanding contributions to research. Dr. Marcia McNutt is president.

The **National Academy of Engineering** was established in 1964 under the charter of the National Academy of Sciences to bring the practices of engineering to advising the nation. Members are elected by their peers for extraordinary contributions to engineering. Dr. C. D. Mote, Jr., is president.

The **National Academy of Medicine** (formerly the Institute of Medicine) was established in 1970 under the charter of the National Academy of Sciences to advise the nation on medical and health issues. Members are elected by their peers for distinguished contributions to medicine and health. Dr. Victor J. Dzau is president.

The three Academies work together as the **National Academies of Sciences, Engineering, and Medicine** to provide independent, objective analysis and advice to the nation and conduct other activities to solve complex problems and inform public policy decisions. The National Academies also encourage education and research, recognize outstanding contributions to knowledge, and increase public understanding in matters of science, engineering, and medicine.

Learn more about the National Academies of Sciences, Engineering, and Medicine at **www.national-academies.org**.

The National Academies of
SCIENCES • ENGINEERING • MEDICINE

Consensus Study Reports published by the National Academies of Sciences, Engineering, and Medicine document the evidence-based consensus on the study's statement of task by an authoring committee of experts. Reports typically include findings, conclusions, and recommendations based on information gathered by the committee and the committee's deliberations. Each report has been subjected to a rigorous and independent peer-review process and it represents the position of the National Academies on the statement of task.

Proceedings published by the National Academies of Sciences, Engineering, and Medicine chronicle the presentations and discussions at a workshop, symposium, or other event convened by the National Academies. The statements and opinions contained in proceedings are those of the participants and are not endorsed by other participants, the planning committee, or the National Academies.

For information about other products and activities of the National Academies, please visit www.nationalacademies.org/about/whatwedo.

STEERING COMMITTEE ON UNDERSTANDING STRATEGIC REASONING FOR NATIONAL SECURITY PURPOSES: A WORKSHOP

GREG TREVERTON (*Chair*), Dornsife College of Letters, Arts, and Sciences, School of International Relations, University of Southern California
ANDREW BENNETT, Walsh School of Foreign Service, Georgetown University
SUMIT GANGULY, Department of Political Science, Indiana University, Bloomington
JUDITH KELLEY, Sanford School of Public Policy, Duke University
JEFFREY TALIAFERRO, Department of Political Science, Tufts University

SUJEETA BHATT, *Study Director*
ELIZABETH TOWNSEND, *Research Associate*
RENÉE L. WILSON, *Senior Program Assistant*

COMMITTEE ON A DECADAL SURVEY OF SOCIAL AND BEHAVIORAL SCIENCES FOR APPLICATIONS TO NATIONAL SECURITY

PAUL R. SACKETT (*Chair*), Department of Psychology, University of Minnesota
GARY G. BERNTSON, Department of Psychology, The Ohio State University
KATHLEEN M. CARLEY, School of Computer Science, Institute for Software Research International, Carnegie Mellon University
NOSHIR S. CONTRACTOR, McCormick School of Engineering and Applied Science, School of Communications, and the Kellogg School of Management, Northwestern University
NANCY J. COOKE, The Polytechnic School, Fulton Schools of Engineering, Arizona State University
BARBARA ANNE DOSHER, Department of Cognitive Science, University of California, Irvine
JEFFREY C. JOHNSON, Department of Anthropology, University of Florida
SALLIE KELLER, Biocomplexity Institute, Virginia Polytechnic Institute and State University, National Capital Region
DAVID MATSUMOTO, Department of Psychology, College of Science and Engineering, San Francisco State University
CARMEN MEDINA, MedinAnalytics, LLC
FRAN P. MOORE, CENTRA Technology, Inc.
JONATHAN D. MORENO, Perelman School of Medicine, Department of Medical Ethics and Health Policy, University of Pennsylvania
JOY ROHDE, Gerald R. Ford School of Public Policy, University of Michigan
JEFFREY W. TALIAFERRO, Department of Political Science, Tufts University
GREGORY F. TREVERTON, Dornsife College of Letters, Arts, and Sciences, School of International Relations, University of Southern California
JEREMY M. WOLFE, Brigham and Women's Hospital, Departments of Ophthalmology and Radiology, Harvard Medical School

SUJEETA BHATT, *Study Director*
ALEXANDRA BEATTY, *Senior Program Officer*
JULIE ANNE SCHUCK, *Program Officer*
ELIZABETH TOWNSEND, *Research Associate*
RENÉE L. WILSON GAINES, *Senior Program Assistant*

BOARD ON BEHAVIORAL, COGNITIVE, AND SENSORY SCIENCES

SUSAN T. FISKE (*Chair*), Department of Psychology and Woodrow Wilson School of Public and International Affairs, Princeton University
JOHN BAUGH, Department of Arts & Sciences, Washington University in St. Louis
LAURA L. CARSTENSEN, Department of Psychology, Stanford University
JUDY DUBNO, Department of Otolaryngology-Head and Neck Surgery, Medical University of South Carolina
JENNIFER EBERHARDT, Department of Psychology, Stanford University
ROBERT L. GOLDSTONE, Department of Psychological and Brain Sciences, Indiana University
DANIEL R. ILGEN, Department of Psychology, Michigan State University
JAMES S. JACKSON, Institute for Social Research, University of Michigan
NANCY G. KANWISHER, Department of Brain and Cognitive Sciences, Massachusetts Institute of Technology
JANICE KIECOLT-GLASER, Department of Psychology, The Ohio State University College of Medicine
BILL C. MAURER, School of Social Sciences, University of California, Irvine
JOHN MONAHAN, School of Law, University of Virginia
STEVEN E. PETERSEN, Department of Neurology and Neurological Surgery, Washington University School of Medicine
DANA M. SMALL, Department of Psychiatry, Yale Medical School
TIMOTHY J. STRAUMAN, Department of Psychology and Neuroscience, Duke University
JEREMY M. WOLFE, Brigham and Women's Hospital, Departments of Ophthalmology and Radiology, Harvard Medical School

BARBARA A. WANCHISEN, *Director*
THELMA COX, *Program Coordinator*

Acknowledgments

This Proceedings of a Workshop was reviewed in draft form by individuals chosen for their diverse perspectives and technical expertise. The purpose of this independent review is to provide candid and critical comments that will assist the National Academies of Sciences, Engineering, and Medicine in making each published proceedings as sound as possible and to ensure that it meets the institutional standards for quality, objectivity, evidence, and responsiveness to the charge. The review comments and draft manuscript remain confidential to protect the integrity of the process.

We thank the following individuals for their review of this proceedings: Richard Cincotta, Global Political Demography Program, The Stimson Center; Nichole Argo Ben Itzhak, Social and Decision Sciences, Carnegie Mellon University; and Sumit Ganguly, Department of Political Science, Indiana University.

Although the reviewers listed above provided many constructive comments and suggestions, they were not asked to endorse the content of the proceedings, nor did they see the final draft before its release. The review of this proceedings was overseen by Philip E. Rubin, Haskins Laboratories. He was responsible for making certain that an independent examination of this proceedings was carried out in accordance with standards of the National Academies and that all review comments were carefully considered. Responsibility for the final content rests entirely with the rapporteur and the National Academies.

Greg Treverton, *Chair*
Steering Committee on Emerging Trends and Methods in
International Security

Contents

1 **INTRODUCTION**   1
   The Decadal Survey of Social and Behavioral Sciences for
      Applications to National Security, 1
   Objectives for the Six Workshops, 3
   Introduction to the Workshop on Emerging Trends and Methods
      in International Security, 4
   Structure of This Proceedings, 5

2 **STATUS, POWER, AND REPUTATION**   7
   Status in International Security, 7
   Shifting Power and the Legitimacy of the International
      Pecking Order, 9
   Measuring Reputation, Power, and Status in Nonstate Actors, 11
   Remarks from Suzanne Fry, 14
   Discussion, 15

3 **STRATEGIC USE OF INFORMATION**   17
   Cyber-Enabled Information Warfare and Influence Operations, 17
   Internet Content, Information Conflict, and the Future of
      Free Expression, 20
   Cyber Persistence: Rethinking Security and Seizing the Strategic
      Cyber Initiative, 24
   Remarks from Suzanne Fry, 25
   Discussion, 27

4 FORECASTING METHODS AND TOPICS 29
From Prediction to Practice: Integrating Forecasting
  Models into Public Health Education and Response, 29
Forecasting Water Availability in Arid Regions, 32
Authoritarian Backsliding: Drivers, Trends, and Implications, 36
Connecting Theory to Policy with Forecasting, 38
Remarks from Suzanne Fry, 42
Discussion, 43

5 TRENDS IN SOCIAL SCIENCE METHODS 47

6 CLOSING THOUGHTS 51
Missing Topics, 51
Workshop Themes, 53

APPENDIXES

A Statement of Task for the Decadal Survey of Social and
  Behavioral Sciences for Applications to National Security 57
B Workshop Agenda 59
C Participants List 63
D Biographical Sketches of Steering Committee and Presenters 69

1

Introduction

The Office of the Director of National Intelligence (ODNI), which oversees and directs the work of the 17 agencies and organizations responsible for foreign, military, and domestic intelligence for the United States, has a growing interest in research from the social and behavioral sciences that may be beneficial to the Intelligence Community (IC). To develop a systematic understanding of these potential benefits, ODNI requested that the National Academies of Sciences, Engineering, and Medicine conduct a decadal survey of the social and behavioral sciences to identify research opportunities that show promise for supporting national security efforts in the next 10 years.

THE DECADAL SURVEY OF SOCIAL AND BEHAVIORAL SCIENCES FOR APPLICATIONS TO NATIONAL SECURITY

A decadal survey is a method for engaging members of a research community to identify lines of research with the greatest potential utility in the pursuit of a particular goal. The National Academies pioneered this type of survey with a study of ground-based astronomy in 1964.[1] Since then, committees appointed by the National Academies have conducted more than 15 decadal surveys. The Decadal Survey of Social and Behavioral Sciences for Applications to National Security represents the first opportunity to apply this approach to the social and behavioral sciences.

---

[1] National Academy of Sciences. (1964). *Ground-Based Astronomy: A Ten-Year Program*. Washington, DC: National Academy Press. doi: https://doi.org/10.17226/13212 [April 2018].

Its purpose is to develop an understanding of the lines of research in these fields that offer the greatest potential to enhance the capabilities of the IC. To carry out this work, the National Academies appointed the Committee on the Decadal Survey of Social and Behavioral Sciences for Applications to National Security (Decadal Survey Committee); the committee's charge appears in Appendix A.

The Decadal Survey Committee has pursued many avenues in collecting information about the needs of the IC and relevant cutting-edge research in the social and behavioral sciences. As part of its information-gathering process, the committee held a series of six workshops—the first three on October 11, 2017, and the second three on January 24, 2018. These workshops, for which planning began early in the committee process, were designed to explore areas about which the committee wished to learn more and to allow the committee to engage with a broad range of experts. The topics selected for the workshops do not necessarily indicate the ultimate direction of the committee's deliberations.[2] The six topics addressed by the workshops were

1. changing sociocultural dynamics and implications for national security;
2. emerging trends and methods in international security;
3. leveraging advances in social network thinking for national security;
4. learning from the science of cognition and perception for decision making;
5. workforce development and intelligence analysis; and
6. understanding narratives for national security purposes.

Separate steering committees, whose membership included both members of the Decadal Survey Committee and additional experts in the topics to be addressed, were appointed to plan these workshops. Each of these committees was guided by its own charge. All were asked to bring their expertise to bear in identifying specific areas of promising research and experts with deep knowledge who could offer a range of insights.

This proceedings of a workshop, prepared by the workshop rapporteur, summarizes the presentations and discussions at the second workshop, on emerging trends and methods in international security. This workshop was planned by the Steering Committee on Understanding Strategic Reasoning for National Security Purposes, whose charge is presented in Box 1-1. The workshop's purpose was to explore the current state of research on political

---

[2] For more information about the Decadal Survey and all of the workshops, see http://sites.nationalacademies.org/dbasse/bbcss/sbs_for_national_security-decadal_survey/index.htm [January 2018].

> **BOX 1-1**
> **Workshop Steering Committee Charge**
>
> An ad hoc committee will plan and conduct a 1-day public workshop. The workshop will feature invited presentations and discussions to review the current state of science on political and strategic reasoning, both traditional and alternative perspectives, with a focus on examining the role of political or economic actors, structures, and/or contexts within which they exist (e.g., domestic, international, transnational). The workshop will explore the varied methods or techniques to discern between correlation and causation. The committee will plan and organize the workshop, select speakers and discussants, and moderate the discussions at the workshop. The workshop will be part of a set of workshops designed to gather information for the Decadal Survey of Social and Behavioral Sciences for Applications to National Security. Proceedings of the workshop will be prepared by a designated rapporteur in accordance with institutional guidelines.

and strategic reasoning in the context of international security. It should be noted that the steering committee's role was limited to planning and convening the workshop, and that the views contained in this proceedings are those of individual workshop participants and do not necessarily represent the views of all workshop participants, the steering committee, or the National Academies.[3] The agenda for the workshop appears in Appendix B; a list of individuals who attended the three workshops held on October 11, 2017, is presented in Appendix C; and biographical sketches of the steering committee members and speakers are provided in Appendix D.

OBJECTIVES FOR THE SIX WORKSHOPS

In an opening session for the three October 11, 2017, workshops, the chair of the Decadal Survey Committee, Paul Sackett, University of Minnesota, and sponsor representative David Honey, ODNI, provided background information on the objectives for the six workshops.

Sackett observed that the Decadal Survey Committee will rely heavily on input from experts in the communities of national security and behavioral and social science research. Given the breadth of the committee's charge, he explained, it must cast a wide net, extending well beyond the specific expertise of its members. He described the six workshops as an

---

[3] For the archived Webcast of the workshop and available presentations, see http://sites.nationalacademies.org/DBASSE/BBCSS/DBASSE_181267 [November 2017].

important part of the effort to gather ideas. The workshops would support the committee by helping to identify promising research areas and allowing the committee members to engage in discussion with experts in a wide range of areas salient to its work.[4]

Honey expressed appreciation to all those contributing to the committee's work through the workshops and other activities, noting that the participation of the full range of experts in the intelligence and behavioral and social science communities would be needed to make the decadal study successful. Making predictions about future directions for research is difficult, he acknowledged, but in his view it is necessary. He noted that the final report of the Decadal Survey Committee will be "a very powerful tool" for government officials who must make decisions regarding funding and other priorities. The decadal model, he explained, "offered the best opportunity" to identify research directions and priorities that reflect a wide range of insights and perspectives. "Decision makers are really asking much deeper and more probing questions today than we've seen before," he said. "They really want to know why surprising movements such as the Arab Spring [uprisings that began in 2010] occur. The national security community is eager for new ways to understand such events and how to respond to them, and also for better ways to assess their interventions after the fact." Honey thanked the participants for contributing, emphasizing that their ideas would be "crucial for getting us where we need to go."

INTRODUCTION TO THE WORKSHOP ON EMERGING TRENDS AND METHODS IN INTERNATIONAL SECURITY

Consequential actors in international relations are growing in both number and diversity, noted steering committee chair Jeffrey Taliaferro, Tufts University, in opening the workshop. While complex and substantive issues continue to present new challenges, he said, the field of international security has evolved to embrace numerous academic disciplines, theoretical schools, methodologies, and ontologies. Thus, he explained, the workshop was planned as an opportunity for discussion with experts from a variety of domains. He added that the steering committee invited experts to explore three areas that shed light on both issues and methods in the international security arena: the changing nature and international security implications of status, power, and reputation among state and nonstate actors; cyber policy and security; and methods of forecasting negative developments with security implications. For the discussion of forecasting, the steering committee sought to examine approaches used in disparate domains, including

---

[4] For more information on activities associated with the Decadal Survey, see http://nas.edu/SBSDecadalSurvey.

public health and the environment. Taliaferro acknowledged that a 1-day workshop could not begin to address the full range of current international security challenges, but explained that the presentations and discussions would allow participants to examine possible links across domains.

STRUCTURE OF THIS PROCEEDINGS

This proceedings follows the structure of the workshop. Chapter 2 summarizes the workshop presentations and discussions on the changing nature of status, power, and reputation. Chapter 3 turns to the strategic use of information, summarizing presentations and discussions on cyber-enabled information warfare and influence operations, Internet regulation under authoritarian governments, and the use of strategic cyber persistence. Chapter 4 explores forecasting methods and topics. Chapter 5 reviews trends in social science methods relevant to intelligence analysis. Finally, Chapter 6 includes the reflections of a panel of distinguished scholars on the presentations summarized in Chapters 2 through 5.

2

Status, Power, and Reputation

Presentations in the first workshop session addressed the international security implications of status, power, and reputation among both state and nonstate actors. Suzanne Fry of the National Intelligence Council (NIC) then offered reflections on the presentations and suggested topics for research that would benefit the Intelligence Community (IC). The panel closed with an open discussion between the presenters and audience members.

STATUS IN INTERNATIONAL SECURITY

Observing that "status" is commonly defined as an actor's position in a social hierarchy, Steven Ward, Cornell University, provided an overview of how this phenomenon applies to states in the context of international politics. He reviewed the way the term is used by researchers, presented some key findings from emerging research in this area, and offered his ideas about future research directions.

For a state, Ward explained, status could mean membership in an elite club of states, such as the great powers or the West, or rank in an ordered list. Status cannot be achieved unilaterally, he added: a state's position in the hierarchy must be granted by others through active accommodation. Furthermore, for status to be meaningful, it must be recognized by other relevant actors.

Status, Ward continued, overlaps with the concepts of power and reputation, but there are important differences. A state with power, he elaborated, has influence over outcomes because of its material capabilities; power is not dependent on the recognition of others. Thus, he said, a state can satisfy its ambition for more power without having to convince others that the ambition is legitimate. Ward acknowledged that some scholars view the boundary between status and power as less distinct because status produces influence, which in turn is a kind of power. In any case, he added, status hierarchies are shaped by the distribution of power in the international system.

Like status, reputation also depends on the assessment of other actors regarding the value of a state's attributes, Ward explained. But because status refers to a state's position in a social hierarchy, he continued, one state's gain generally corresponds to a loss for others—a phenomenon that does not apply to reputation. Moreover, whereas reputation is valued primarily as a tool that can be used for leverage in the international system, the acquisition of status is often regarded as a foreign policy objective.

"What justifies the growing focus on status among analysts of international politics?" Ward asked rhetorically. He observed that recognition of status as an important driver in international politics can be traced back at least to the 5th-century historian Thucydides. The current interest in status, he suggested, reflects insights from such fields as behavioral economics and social psychology, which have amassed a significant amount of empirical evidence showing that human beings care about their standing and the standing of the groups to which they belong.

According to Ward, researchers have established both that states care about their own status and that concerns about status have their own influence on foreign policy apart from issues of security and power. This point might seem trivial, he acknowledged, but researchers have demonstrated that this intangible phenomenon can make a difference in international politics. Rising powers are especially sensitive to status concerns, he added. He explained that, although scholars do not necessarily agree on the reason for this sensitivity, it has long been understood that unsatisfied status ambitions and disruptive foreign policies are strongly linked. Researchers have also explored ways in which states seek status through both violent and peaceful means. As an example of the latter, Ward pointed to the positive association between Olympic medal performance and the accumulation of diplomatic ties (such ties are used as a quantitative measure of status).

Ward then turned to important questions about status that remain unanswered. First, he said, although rising powers are known to prize international status, little is known about how status concerns affect other types of states, such as small states. Such research, he asserted, would be useful in understanding how status concerns may be implicated in disputes, such as that between Qatar and other Gulf states. Another unanswered question, he continued, is whether status has any instrumental value. While it is assumed that high status induces deference in other states, he elaborated, there is no evidence to prove this assumption is true. He views this as an important question for policy makers who may be wondering about the extent to which they should be concerned about status abroad. Next, he pointed out that, although it is well known that states care about status, scholars do not yet understand why. This is another area, he argued, that has been characterized by assumptions rather than evidence. Perhaps the most important policy implication from recent work on status, he suggested, is that "a great deal of conflict could be avoided if established powers were willing to accommodate the status ambitions of rising powers." However, he added, researchers have not systematically established what accommodation is and how it works, so it is impossible to say, for instance, "what American accommodation of Chinese status ambitions should look like, or what its costs might be."

Ward closed by offering his expectations for future research in this area. He anticipates that new experimental work will test theories of status related to individual attitudes and behaviors, and also develop improved quantitative measures of status. He also expects to see more research on the role of status anxiety among regional or middle powers and states facing relative decline, and on the links between international status and domestic politics. Research on status, he cautioned, is vital because "status concerns might be . . . wrapped up in questions about regime vulnerability and nuclear proliferation in places like North Korea and Iran."

SHIFTING POWER AND THE LEGITIMACY OF THE INTERNATIONAL PECKING ORDER

Social identity theory is a tool for understanding reputation, power, and legitimacy in the international system, observed Deborah Larson, University of California, Los Angeles. This theory, she explained, accounts for people's behavior through a focus on their social identity, that part of their self-concept that is derived from being a member of a social group. When people's self-image is closely tied to a group, she continued, they want that group to be viewed as superior and distinctive relative to other groups. Individuals experience their group's triumphs and defeats as if they were their own, and they evaluate their group's status by comparing it with that of a reference group that is similar but slightly higher in rank. For example, it is likely that Russia and China compare themselves with the United States, India compares itself with China, and France compares itself with Germany.

Larson continued by observing that groups (such as states) that regard themselves as having lower relative status may use identity management strategies to improve their ranking. One such strategy, she said, is to pursue social mobility. Thus a state may hope to gain membership in an elite group by following recognized rules and improving its standing on valued attributes. For example, Larson noted, at the end of the Cold War, central and eastern European states withdrew from the Warsaw Pact and adopted democracy and liberal capitalism to gain entry into the North Atlantic Treaty Organization (NATO) and the European Union (EU), which were considered to have higher status.

A second strategy for improving relative status, Larson continued, is social competition, used when a group strives to equal or surpass a dominant group. This strategy may be used, she explained, when a group believes that the boundaries of the dominant group are impermeable and that the status hierarchy is illegitimate or unstable. For example, she said, a status hierarchy would be considered illegitimate if high-ranking members were perceived as having double standards or bullying other states. And an indicator that a status hierarchy was unstable would be if lower-status powers were consistently demanding greater influence over the rules and norms of the international system.

Larson explained that, in this geopolitical version of social competition, a challenger state will compete with elite groups over allies, client states, and weaponry. This situation can lead to conflict, she asserted, if other states see the challenger state as a threat. She added that, if the challenger state is not powerful enough to surpass the dominant state, it will act as a spoiler by trying to humiliate the higher-status state or prevent it from attaining its goals. She cited Russia as a current example, suggesting that it is acting as a spoiler because it lacks the military or economic power to overcome the United States, although its leader, Vladimir Putin, perceives the status hierarchy as illegitimate because Russia is not included as a leading power.

A third strategy for elevating the status of a state, according to Larson, is social creativity, which can take two forms. First, a state may seek to change the perception of a trait traditionally seen as negative. Larson cited the example of Xi Jinping, the leader of China, who promotes Confucianism, a philosophy once criticized by the communist leader Mao Zedong. She added that China has also demonstrated the social creativity strategy through its policy of pursuing increased power without posing a threat to other countries. Alternatively, she continued, a state may attempt to excel in a new dimension, as did former Soviet leader Mikhail Gorbachev. Gorbachev "used social creativity in his attempt to achieve preeminence for the Soviet Union as leader of a New World Order based on . . . new thinking [about] . . . mutual security, nonuse of force, and nonoffensive defense," she explained. This approach to social creativity is used, she elaborated, when the dominant group is impermeable, while the existing status hierarchy is believed to be stable (change in the hierarchy is unlikely) and legitimate (its norms are considered fair). However, she noted, if the dominant state refuses to recognize the new dimension as valuable or the aspiring state as superior on that dimension, social creativity is not effective.

Larson emphasized that a state using social creativity must have a minimum level of "hard power," or military capability. As with social competition, she observed, a state's attempt at social creativity can result in conflict. She asserted that examination of the above strategies for challenging international hierarchies demonstrates how international stability depends on two factors. First, if aspiring powers are to continue to believe in the stability of the current status hierarchy, she explained, the United States must maintain its overall superiority. However, she added, aspiring powers must also perceive that is it possible for them to be admitted into an elite group if the status hierarchy is to maintain its legitimacy.

Larson closed by sharing her thoughts on future research. She noted that a number of researchers are studying status among rising powers, such as India, Brazil, and Turkey, and reiterated Ward's assertion that more research is needed on the uses and limitations of status incentives. She added that research is also needed to understand how the status ambitions of smaller states, such as the Balkans, Serbia, and Montenegro, can be accommodated within the current system. Finally, she called attention to the increasing interest in trust and trusting relationships. For example, she noted, mistrust is often an obstacle to resolving disagreements between states. Accordingly, she suggested, it is important to understand the modalities of building trust and what kind of institutional arrangements might substitute for trust.

MEASURING REPUTATION, POWER, AND STATUS IN NONSTATE ACTORS

Observing that reputation, power, and trust are also important for nonstate actors, Amanda Murdie, University of Georgia, explored how these phenomena can be measured in the context of such groups. The term "nonstate actors," she explained, encompasses "good guys," such as nongovernmental organizations (NGOs), including, for example, Amnesty International and Greenpeace, and traditional "bad guys," such as terrorist groups, drug cartels, and rebel groups. She added that individuals, such as Angelina Jolie and Leonardo DiCaprio, who play a role in international affairs are also considered nonstate actors. She clarified, however, that the term does not encompass states or organizations established by states, such as government-organized nongovernmental organizations (GONGOs); intergovernmental organizations (IGOs); or organizations and individuals representing political parties.

Murdie explained further that nonstate actors can also be distinguished by whether they are (1) typically violent or nonviolent, or (2) for-profit or not-for-profit. She illustrated this point with a two-by-two table, which demonstrates these divisions for such nonstate actors as drug cartels (typi-

		Profit	
		For Profit	Not-for-Profit
Violence	Violent	Criminal Organizations, Drug Cartels	Terrorist Groups, Rebel Groups
	Nonviolent	Businesses, MNCs	NGOs, Religious Organizations, Universities

FIGURE 2-1 Categories of nonstate actors.
NOTE: MNCs = multinational corporations, NGOs = nongovernmental organizations.
SOURCE: Created by Amanda Murdie for the workshop.

cally violent and for-profit) and NGOs (typically nonviolent and not-for-profit) (see Figure 2-1). According to Murdie, it is generally accepted that nonstate actors have a central toolkit they leverage to affect foreign policy and international security. However, she said, the distinctions displayed in Figure 2-1 can be blurred when organizations change tactics to effect change. For example, she elaborated, an actor that is nonviolent and not-for-profit in one situation may use a different tool in another.

Murdie analyzed data derived from the Teaching and Research on International Policy (TRIP) survey to develop an overview of the research on nonstate actors. This survey, initiated in 2003, is examining connections among teaching, research, and policy in international relations.[1] Murdie explained that the developers of the survey also maintain a database of coded publications in leading international relations and political science journals from 1980 to 2015. She found that 10 percent of all articles included in the survey are focused on nonstate actors. Although this is a small percentage, she emphasized that interest in nonstate actors has grown significantly since 1980. There has also been an increase in quantitative research methods and systematic measurement since 2008, she observed. However, she added, despite recent work on terrorist groups, NGOs, and religious organizations, the influence of violent for-profit organizations and individual nonstate actors on international security has been largely ignored.

One method of measuring nonstate actors, Murdie noted, is to count the number of organizations. While this may appear to be a straightforward method, she said, organizations working in repressive regimes frequently change their names to stay under the radar. Another research approach is

---

[1] For more information on the TRIP survey, see https://trip.wm.edu/home/index.php/about-us/what-we-do [January 2018].

to measure the outputs of such groups, although the nature of their outputs varies. For example, Murdie explained, the output for a nonviolent, not-for-profit organization might be the dissemination of a product, such as a press release or report, whereas the output for a terrorist organization might be the number of terrorist events or the lethality of those events. She added that the level of media attention these outputs receive is an indicator of status, power, and reputation.

Murdie has also explored how the status, power, and reputation of nonstate actors are perceived by others in their community, as well as by outside actors, such as states and IGOs. Some large, prominent NGOs, she noted, have sufficient status that they can act as gatekeepers on the international stage and help determine which issues receive international attention.[2] Other groups may claim connections to higher-status organizations as a way of increasing their own stature.

Murdie closed with a look at possible trends in future research. She suggested that big data and advanced machine learning techniques, which are increasingly accessible to researchers, should be used to evaluate well-known, but untested, theories. In her view, more research is needed on the international significance of violent, for-profit criminal organizations, as well as on individual nonstate actors, such as celebrity activists and religious leaders. She also hopes that researchers will focus on nonstate actors that transition from violent to nonviolent methods. She added that a new dataset, NAVCO 2.0,[3] which tracks violent and nonviolent campaigns and changes in their tactics over time, would be a valuable resource for such work.

Nonstate actors have a growing role in complex emergencies and counterinsurgencies, Murdie noted, and it is not uncommon for military actors, NGOs, and rebel groups to be in contact during conflicts. She suggested that research is needed to understand how status, power, and reputation are affected by these complex relationships.

Finally, Murdie pointed out that, since the terrorist attacks of September 11, 2001, there has been a steady decline in civil society, by which she meant the influence of NGOs and similar social organizations. States may intend to prevent funding from reaching terrorists through nonstate actor networks, she noted, but some countries are taking the opportunity to restrict even groups that operate on a strictly neutral humanitarian level. She

---

[2] Carpenter, R. (2010). Governing the global agenda: "Gatekeepers" and "issue adoption" in transnational advocacy networks. In D. Avant, M. Finnemore, and S. Sell (Eds.), *Who Governs the Globe?* (Cambridge Studies in International Relations, pp. 202–237). Cambridge, UK: Cambridge University Press. doi:10.1017/CBO9780511845369.009.

[3] For more information on the University of Denver's Nonviolent and Violent Campaigns and Outcomes (NAVCO) Data Project, see https://www.du.edu/korbel/sie/research/chenow_navco_data.html [January 2018].

suggested that research is needed to understand the factors that have led to such crackdowns and how they are affecting nonstate actors.

REMARKS FROM SUZANNE FRY

Fry began her reflections on the three presentations of this panel by introducing the audience to the NIC's quadrennial *Global Trends*[4] series, an unclassified publication aimed at assessing the implications of global trends and uncertainties. She reported that this publication has documented an increase in the number and diversity of actors benefiting from the diffusion of power. States, she observed, used to be the primary holders of power, but analysts are now seeing power diffuse to nonstate actors, such as organizations and individuals.

To address the implications of this change, Fry argued, scholars should consider developing theories that take into account multiple types of actors, including IGOs and political parties. She seconded Murdie's suggestion that theories are needed to examine the disruptive effects of understudied violent, for-profit groups, such as drug trafficking organizations. She also agreed with Larson that social identity theory can help researchers understand the strategic choices such actors make. However, she cautioned that researchers should not limit the application of their theories to a single scenario. Unlike analysts, she noted, researchers do not have the benefit of having access to all-source information, a limitation that could cause them to be guided by inaccurate assumptions. Thus, she urged researchers to apply their theories across a range of scenarios. Moreover, she suggested that in considering such issues as status, researchers should look across cultures.

In Fry's view, theories that "seek to explain how these various actors affect outcomes that matter for national security" should also be a high priority for researchers. She observed that many in the IC speculate that nonviolent nonstate actors, such as faith-based charities and Human Rights Watch, play a significant role in the international system, but that evidence demonstrating specific outcomes, such as a reduction or increase in violence, is needed to validate this hypothesis. Similarly, she suggested that, rather than thinking about power in relation to capability, researchers should think about power in relation to outcomes. While such attributes as military size or population size are important, she said, it is also critical that researchers explain what outcomes are associated with these attributes. She noted that in real-world applications of theory, analysts will often combine multiple theories to understand changes in the geopolitical landscape. Thus, she concluded, using case study research to review significant moments of

---

[4] For more information on the NIC's *Global Trends*, see https://www.dni.gov/index.php/global-trends-home [January 2018].

political change and test the explanatory power of various theories in those moments could be helpful to analysts.

DISCUSSION

Workshop participants raised several questions related to status. One question was how status-seeking behavior within nonstate actor organizations compares with that of states. Murdie responded that some public administration research has looked at status within NGOs. However, she noted, less research has examined the internal relationships in terrorist and rebel groups. In particular, she suggested, more research is needed to understand where terrorist and rebel leaders get their power.

Another participant questioned how much researchers know about variations in status concerns across states. Ward and Larson suggested that status concerns are often a mix of historical status and identity. For example, Larson noted, for thousands of years there was no rival to China's power. Ward agreed, and added that, although this is no longer the case, China is still very sensitive to status because there was a time when it was the leader in terms of status and power. Furthermore, Larson observed, countries that are in proximity to one another, such as China, Japan, and India or Brazil and Argentina, will often develop rivalries as a result of culture and history. Murdie added that terrorist organizations are also sensitive to status. After an attack, she noted, leaders will scour media sources to see how many times their group is mentioned in relation to the attack. Ward followed up on Murdie's point by suggesting that more research is needed to understand variations in status among individual actors.

One participant asked how to distinguish between status and prestige. Ward and Larson responded that they have differing views on this topic. Ward defines prestige as reputation for power, whereas status is culturally contextual and can be based on things other than power. Larson, on the other hand, sees prestige as "any sort of quality that the international community values," while status is hierarchical. "You don't talk about somebody having first-class prestige or second-class prestige," she said, "but you do talk about first-class and second-class powers."

A participant asked whether the panelists could identify examples in which only status could explain an outcome. Ward responded that German battleship building before World War I and the 1933 departure of Japan from the League of Nations both evolved from status-seeking behavior.

A final question concerned how status is disputed or conferred among states. A participant wondered whether the status hierarchy could become permeable if a dominant state were to guide a lesser state on relevant issues, and what might be learned about this from the transition of power from Britain to the United States over the course of the 19th and 20th centuries. Larson responded that accommodation depends largely on whether the dominant state is powerful enough to impose its views on a state with lesser status. However, she added, more research is needed to answer this question. With regard to British accommodation of the United States, she suggested that the transition of power from Britain to the United States was not necessarily a smooth one. Britain did not accept that its status had been reduced, she argued, until the 1956 crisis over the Suez Canal.

3

Strategic Use of Information

Presenters in this panel brought three different perspectives to bear on cyber policy and security. Herb Lin, Stanford University, discussed cyber-enabled information warfare and influence operations; Jacklyn Kerr, also of Stanford University, examined Internet regulation in authoritarian governments; and Richard Harknett, University of Cincinnati, addressed the use of strategic cyber persistence. Suzanne Fry, National Intelligence Council, then offered comments on these presentations and their implications for future research. The panel closed with an open discussion between presenters and audience members.

CYBER-ENABLED INFORMATION WARFARE AND INFLUENCE OPERATIONS

Lin framed his presentation with the question, "What would Hitler have been able to do with the Internet?" Information warfare and influence operations, he explained, denote the "deliberate use of information to confuse, mislead, and affect the choices and decisions" of an adversary. Although hostile, he added, they do not represent warfare in the traditional sense as defined by the United Nations Charter or laws of armed conflict. Noting the juxtaposition between the terms "information," which implies propaganda and persuasion, and "warfare," which suggests armed conflict, he quoted Sun-Tzu, author of *The Art of War*: "The supreme art of war is to subdue the enemy without fighting." He noted that cyberwar is categorized as either (1) high-level (crippling society as a whole, attacking critical infrastructure, or destroying weapons systems); or (2) low-level (drug dealing, child pornography, hacktivism, credit card fraud, and theft of intellectual property).

According to Lin, information warfare has "its own battle space and theory of operations." He explained that conflict takes place in the information environment of cyberspace and involves the cognitive and emotional parts of the brain. He added that victory in information warfare and influence operations is when the adversary willingly accepts and adopts the victor's political goals not because the adversary no longer has the means to resist (e.g., if it were militarily defeated), but because the adversary no longer views the victor as the enemy. Knowledge, truth, and confidence are all damaged, he continued, as the result of infection of the adversary's decision process with fear, anger, and uncertainty. Furthermore, he asserted, there are no noncombatants in information warfare and influence operations; everyone, including governments, universities, and news media, is a potential target.

Lin outlined ways in which creating chaos and confusion can be damaging to a state adversary. First, he suggested, it creates conflict and uncertainty in the targeted state, and this internal conflict also harms the state's international reputation. Moreover, he added, a state is unlikely to take action in response to information warfare and influence operations because they fall below the "act of war" threshold. He noted that, if the attacking state chooses to identify itself as responsible for such an act, the act is classified as being a "white" operation; if the identity of the responsible group is unclear, the act is considered a "gray" operation; and if another party is blamed, the act is regarded as a "black" operation.

Lin also described three main types of information warfare and influence operations. The first, propaganda, disseminates false information to influence attitudes and opinions. Information developed to reach a wide audience, Lin explained, often consists of a simple and repeated lie that appeals to emotions rather than reason; he likened this to the approach used in Hitler's *Mein Kampf*. The second type is a chaos-producing operation. With this method, Lin explained, a high volume of false messages, such as trolls' posts about fabricated disasters, is released rapidly to the public. The messages, he noted, need not be consistent or have a purpose. The third type, a leak operation, involves leaking secret and often embarrassing or compromising information to the public.

Lin noted that, while information warfare is old, cyber-enabled information warfare is relatively new and has several advantages. For example, he said, it is inexpensive and easy to disseminate the information to a wide audience. Thus, he added, even small groups can have a loud voice. Moreover, he observed, this form of warfare is often legal and can reach international audiences, and it is not difficult for the attacking actor to remain anonymous. Furthermore, marginalized communities can locate one another and join forces to become more powerful. For example, Lin noted, automated Twitter accounts can amplify messages. He explained that information warfare and influence operations take advantage of the advertised features of information technology, whereas cyberwar takes advantage of the virtues of information technology.

According to Lin, it is human cognitive and emotional biases that help information warfare and influence operations work. To illustrate, he pointed out that fluency bias and illusory truth bias allow simple and repeated messages to be received positively; confirmation bias causes people to seek out only information that is already in line with their beliefs; and emotional bias prevents people with strong emotional beliefs from considering rational arguments.

Lin noted that some interest in policy changes has resulted from Russia's interference with the 2016 presidential election. He asserted that the main consequence of this interference was that it increased political tensions in the United States. However, he added, this would likely have happened regardless of which party won the election. Because of the current polarizing political environment and the nation's poor cyberdefense policies, he argued, the United States is particularly vulnerable to this form of information warfare and influence operations. In his view, moreover, the U.S. military does not always value soft power and often mistrusts people working in information operations.

To respond to information warfare, Lin continued, it is important to identify its targets. If the U.S. government can do a better job of identifying who is being attacked, he suggested, it may be able to do better at identifying when an attack is taking place. Moreover, he argued, for the United States to counter information warfare and influence operations, it must first recognize what will not help. He cited two strategies that are too time consuming to be effective: utilizing "traditional institutions that require coordination" and recruiting "smarter and better-educated people." On the other hand, he suggested, it may help if the United States can drown out the attacking actor with countermessages. He referred to some research indicating that promoting the truth is more effective than attempting to refute false information. He suggested further that the United States may want to initiate more gray operations against perpetrators. He added that the private sector has been working on these issues and should be encouraged to continue those efforts.

Lin also observed that it is especially difficult to use information warfare against authoritarian regimes. Such regimes usually have strict information control systems that limit the types of communication citizens can access.

Lin closed by noting that there have been discussions related to striking a "grand bargain" with U.S. adversaries, according to which the United

States would make concessions in return for an end to information warfare. However, he acknowledged that he is unsure whether this is a real possibility.

INTERNET CONTENT, INFORMATION CONFLICT, AND THE FUTURE OF FREE EXPRESSION

Kerr drew on her work on the Internet and society to argue for continuing research on how authoritarian regimes are evolving in the information age and what the implications are for national and international security. She began by recalling the mass election protests that occurred in Russia in 2011 and 2012, which the country's leadership regarded as an existential threat. She noted that the protesters relied heavily on relatively new information technologies to mobilize fellow citizens, demonstrating the usefulness of these technologies in mass protests.

Kerr added that many people, especially in the West, regarded these new technologies as vital supports for liberty, a tendency she referred to as "cyber utopianism." The Internet allowed people to communicate in ways that were not possible through such traditional channels as print and radio or in media environments that were sometimes highly constrained. However, Kerr noted, authoritarian states threatened by this method of discourse initiated regulations making it more difficult for citizens to communicate freely using the Internet. In response to such authoritarian clampdowns, political figures, such as Hillary Clinton, began publicly advocating for Internet freedom as a democratic freedom and individual right.

These issues have only become more complex in the years since the protests in Russia, Kerr continued. She explained that increases in viral propaganda, extremist content, and hate speech and such developments as the 2016 hack into the Democratic National Committee's computer system have heightened attention to the need for greater Internet security and stability. She believes there is much to be learned from a close look at evolving approaches to the flow of information within authoritarian states.

The Internet has changed dramatically in its short life, Kerr observed. At first, she elaborated, it was regarded as a technology that could not be censored, but by 2010 a variety of technical and nontechnical means for doing just that had been developed. She reported that researchers at The Citizen Lab, a project at the University of Toronto,[1] have measured blocking of content on the Internet and linked it to other forms of repression; their findings are shown in Figure 3-1. The countries on the far right of the figure are the most repressive overall, she explained, but the relationship between censorship and other repression is not always predictable. The

---

[1] For more information, see https://citizenlab.ca [January 2018].

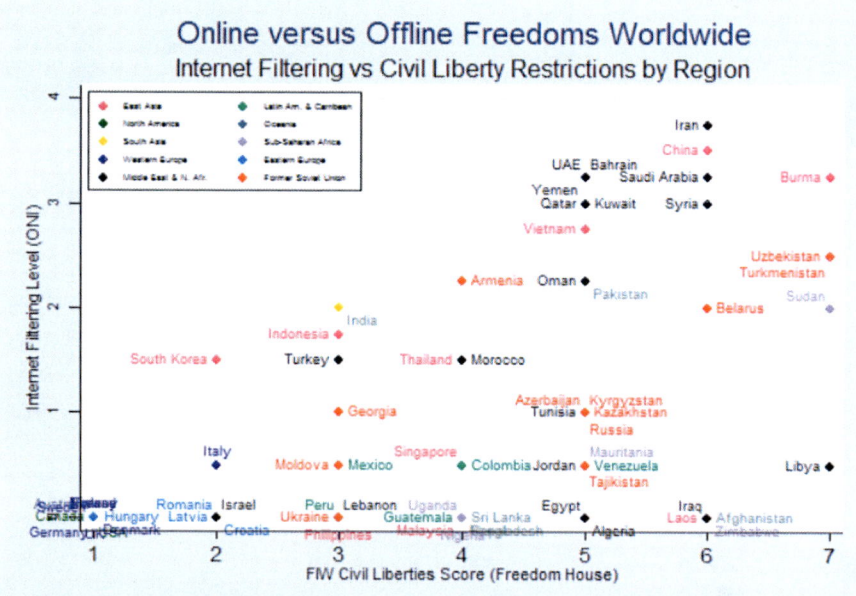

FIGURE 3-1 Links between Internet censorship and other forms of repression.
SOURCE: Kerr, J. (2014). *The Digital Dictator's Dilemma: Internet Regulation and Political Control in Non-Democratic States.* Palo Alto: The Center for International Security and Cooperation, Stanford University. Used with permission.

researchers found, for example, that in some states of the former Soviet Union, there was far greater freedom online than elsewhere in society. How might one account for differences between those states and others, such as China, Qatar, or Saudi Arabia, which adopted more restrictive approaches to the Internet from the outset?

Kerr highlighted two seemingly conflicting trends that shed light on this question. Pointing to Figure 3-2, she explained that, as general Internet penetration increased, the most authoritarian states (shown in red) tended to converge on a norm of relatively high censorship because of the risks they perceived, such as mass protests or regime change. The states with the greatest degree of general freedom, shown in blue, tended to converge in choosing not to censor political and social content on the Internet. In the middle were states that fit neither category and were also relatively late to achieve Internet penetration. These countries, Kerr explained, faced conflicting pressures as they made decisions about censorship. Although they perceived threats in the form of protest movements, they also allowed some democratic freedoms, so they risked being labeled as hypocritical if they violated those freedoms by censoring the Internet.

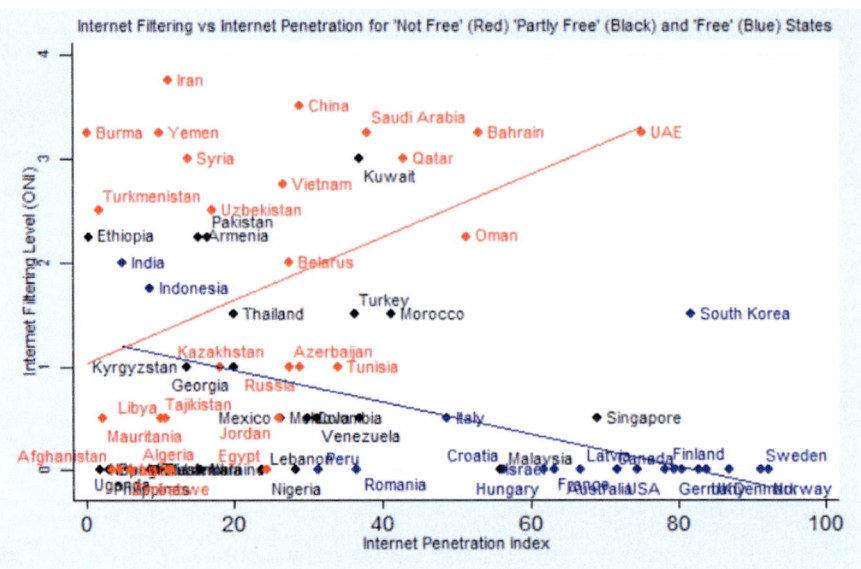

FIGURE 3-2 Online freedom and Internet penetration.
SOURCE: Kerr, J. (2014). *The Digital Dictator's Dilemma: Internet Regulation and Political Control in Non-Democratic States*. Palo Alto: The Center for International Security and Cooperation, Stanford University. Used with permission.

Some of these latter states did impose increased censorship, Kerr continued, but others adapted. She explained that, instead of adopting such overt censorship practices as site blocking and keyword filtering, methods used in the Great Firewall of China since the early 2000s, some countries adopted next-generation approaches that were more subtle and could be denied more plausibly. Table 3-1 lists examples of these two different approaches to censorship. In Russia, for example, Kerr reported that new forms of control over the Internet and information flow included pressure on information technology businesses, improved surveillance capabilities, and the generation of new sorts of targeted content not readily identifiable as propaganda.

Kerr emphasized that these developments blurred the line between censorship and noncensorship, the Chinese and democratic approaches. She acknowledged the spectrum between these two poles, but suggested that limited censorship using less overt tools and in a context of legal and security justifications represents a third approach. The old paradigm, she explained, was of a dichotomy between, on the one hand, a vision of global Internet universalism, according to which access to the Internet is a right and democratic norms of free expression are valued, and, on the other hand, a focus on national cybersecurity with reliance on a range of methods to contain threats. She added that information itself is viewed as a threat to security in Russia and other countries. Russia, she noted, introduced an "information security doctrine" in 2000, just after Vladimir Putin had confronted some very negative publicity about the sinking of a Russian submarine. This doctrine identified both independent Russian media and foreign media as a threat and was part of a gradual media crackdown. The doctrine was updated in 2016 to mention the Internet explicitly, Kerr added.

Similar concepts have been promoted elsewhere, Kerr continued, including in a United Nations code of conduct for information nonaggression. "You see this way of thinking about information being rolled out in military and strategic thought and applications," she commented. Leaks and targeted propaganda, she suggested, are being used as part of toolsets that also include cyberattacks, hacking, and other more technical forms of aggression that are used in domestic and international contexts. The goal of such efforts, she explained, is to exploit the vulnerabilities of groups or coalitions by "changing the narrative, rather than by blocking information." Although those who use these strategies create the illusion that information flows freely, she added, the result is in fact increased control of information.

Kerr identified several pressing research needs in this area. The vulnerability of democratic systems to these new threats needs to be studied, she asserted, and the concept of soft power reexamined in the post–Cold War digital context. She suggested that authoritarian regimes may be more resilient than their democratic counterparts because they have been ad-

TABLE 3-1 Two Approaches to Internet Restriction

"First Generation"	"Next Generation"
Site blocking	Restrictive legal measures
Keyword filtering	Informal takedown requests
Manual censorship of content	Regulation of private companies
Cellular or network shutdowns	Just-in-time blocking/DDoS attacks
Network traffic slowdowns	Patriotic hacking/trolling/blogging
"Walled garden" intranets	Targeted and mass surveillance
	Economic takeovers
	Trials/physical attacks

NOTE: DDoS = distributed denial of service.
SOURCE: Adapted from slide created by Jacklyn Kerr for the workshop.

dressing these issues for 20 years. She also highlighted the need to develop ways of addressing these challenges without violating democratic values. She suggested further that cyberconflict cannot be thoroughly understood through a framework of deterrence and military conflict, arguing that interdisciplinary work incorporating insights from media theory and the study of state–society relations, public opinion, protest movements, government processes, and other relevant areas is needed.

CYBER PERSISTENCE: RETHINKING SECURITY AND SEIZING THE STRATEGIC CYBER INITIATIVE

Harknett began by asking the audience to imagine that it was May 8, 1945, and World War II had just ended. He then argued that all of the tactics, operations, and strategies used to secure that victory would now become secondary. A radical new concept in international security—deterrence—would be needed instead, and it would require the U.S. Congress to spend trillions of dollars on military capabilities that would be developed with the sole purpose of never being used. Although this argument would have seemed outlandish on the day of victory in World War II, Harknett pointed out that this radical new concept was soon accepted.

Harknett used this scenario to illustrate the misalignment between current thinking about security and the realities of cyberconflict. He likened the situation today to paradigm shifts that occur in science, as described by Thomas Kuhn in *The Structure of Scientific Revolutions*, because he believes experts are resisting the implications of the empirical data they are seeing. "If we don't get our fundamental assumptions [about the] strategic environment right," he argued, "then the intelligence requirements, the capabilities that we need to have to do the necessary intelligence to engage in these types of operations are going to be completely out of whack." To demonstrate this strategic misalignment, he pointed to an executive order on cybersecurity recently signed by President Trump, which asks "How are we going to deter?" rather than "How are we going to secure?"

Harknett asserted that, just as the destructive power of nuclear weapons made traditional defense strategies obsolete, the potential dangers of cyberspace make traditional deterrence obsolete. He suggested instead a strategy of cyber persistence, an approach that is not just tactical or operational but also takes into account the capabilities and actions of state and nonstate actors, large and small. He observed that in 1914, for example, it was assumed that going on the offensive provided an advantage, and even the data from the conflict at Verdun during World War I (in which 750,000 casualties were incurred over 10 months for the sake of a quarter-mile advance) did not immediately undermine that assumption.

Turning to defense in a cyber context, Harknett argued that it has little cumulative effect on the overall scale and scope of an adversary's capability. One can remove malware, for example, but the adversary can quickly reengineer it and find a new pathway for its operation.

Neither offense nor defense is particularly helpful in a cyber context, Harknett asserted. Instead, he argued, the focus should be on the interconnectedness of both strategies and organizations, not particular segments of a situation or environment. Cyberspace is not a "war-fighting domain," he suggested, although the military may be viewing it that way. Rather, he said, it is "an interconnected domain in which the military may have to fight." He suggested that national security experts view the situation not as a traditional chess board but as a constantly shifting terrain resembling Figure 3-3.

Harknett concluded his presentation by stating that a focus on cyber persistence has challenging implications for the Intelligence Community (IC). He used wrestling as an analogy to replace the offense/defense framework: "If you come at me and I use your weight as momentum and shift and then pin you, was I playing offense or defense? If I let you into my network or you get into my network but I know you're in my network and I start to follow you, and then use that reconnaissance to understand how I can vector back and take that capability away from you, was I playing offense or defense?" Thus analysts must simultaneously anticipate potential exploitation of vulnerabilities on their side while leveraging the vulnerabilities of adversaries. Those vulnerabilities may not all be technical, Harknett added; as the earlier presentations had suggested, open democratic societies have vulnerabilities that authoritarian ones do not.

In sum, Harknett asserted, cybersecurity will depend on seizing the initiative across the full range of tactics and operations. It will require a "national-level strategy that encompasses resilience, defense, and countercapability in an environment of constant action and universal vulnerability." According to Harknett, the United States must move away from deterrence as the cornerstone strategy for managing cyberspace; it should focus on a strategy of persistence. He believes the need for this shift will only become more pronounced as the next technology leap occurs. He agreed with a statement by Vladimir Putin that whoever controls artificial intelligence will control the future of international dynamics, and noted that China has a grand strategy for translating cyber capabilities and artificial intelligence into strategic advantages, whereas the United States does not.

REMARKS FROM SUZANNE FRY

Fry began her remarks by observing that information has become such a part of the environment that it is like air or water. Thus she suggested that, when researchers think about addressing cyber issues strategically, they "not aim for a cyber grand strategy," but "for a grand strategy given

FIGURE 3-3 Conceptual model of the terrain of cyberspace.
SOURCE: Created by Richard Harknett for the workshop.

an environment in which information is now like oxygen." She stressed the need to understand not just the context of strategy "but actual strategy . . . both in a geopolitical sense as well as in a sort of defensive domestic sense."

Fry agreed with the point made by Lin in his presentation that influence campaigns are driven by emotions. However, she urged researchers to consider how the Internet may be changing the way people feel and behave. She would also like to know how the Internet is used to manipulate people.

Fry observed further that, although information warfare and influence operations are not truly considered warfare in the traditional sense, when taken as a whole they represent attempts by another power to assert dominance. She posed the question, "How do we get our arms around the cumulative effects of this particular tool?" She argued for the need to develop methods with which to measure the effects of information warfare and influence operations, as well as for the need to know whether those effects are marginal or not.

Fry then noted that the military often thinks about an adversary's "center of gravity," which, she said, includes "will to fight, will to support, civic commitment to country," and other "core issues of national loyalty not just among warfighters, but also the citizenry." If the purpose of influence operations is to disrupt the center of gravity, she asserted, researchers need to design ways to measure the outcomes.

According to Fry, another area of interest to the IC is interconnectedness as it relates to the Internet. She pointed out that, although the Internet was created more than two decades ago, little is still known about how it is associated with feelings of peace, love, or tolerance or with fragmentation, conflict, and intolerance. She suggested that more research is needed on this topic.

Turning to Kerr's presentation on authoritarian governments, Fry suggested that it would be helpful if the IC knew how countries decide what information should be blocked. She also wondered whether there is an economic cost to the authoritarian strategy. She suggested that research is needed to determine whether censorship inhibits the ability to accumulate wealth.

Finally, returning to the topic of strategy, Fry suggested that it would be helpful to have "predictions about the patterns of geopolitical competition" and "how those strategies might evolve in the strategic environment."

DISCUSSION

An audience participant opened up the panel discussion by suggesting that cyber issues may be one space in which alliances between state and nonstate actors are likely. Lin responded by noting that when the First Amendment was enacted information was scarce. At the time, he said, it was thought that the "best antidote to bad information is more information." Although access to information is no longer an issue, he continued, the United States is founded on the principle of free speech, which serves to inhibit government action in this area. However, he noted, private industry is not subject to the same constraints as the government. Thus, if there is a solution, he asserted, it will likely be found in the private sector.

Harknett suggested that public–private partnerships are a possibility, but the goals and motives of each partner need to be aligned if progress is to be made. According to Kerr, the Internet has changed the way protesters, bloggers, and other groups communicate and organize in authoritarian governments. She also agreed with Lin's comments about the significance of private-sector actors. There have been moments, she observed, in which public speech has been harmful both to individuals and to society in general. In those moments, she said, private organizations have taken steps to limit speech, a move that changes their role in security issues in democratic settings.

Another topic that arose during the discussion involved interdisciplinary work. An audience member asked what concepts, theories, and methods the fields of political science and security studies should borrow from other disciplines to address cybersecurity issues. Lin replied that the number of disciplines that could work together on these issues is endless. He noted that issues of cybersecurity cut across all fields because "when you're talking about cybersecurity, you're talking about the integrity and reliability of information in every field."

Kerr agreed that a multitude of disciplines could work together on cybersecurity issues. First, she suggested, much can be accomplished with the combination of sociology and big data. She observed that such methods as computational linguistics and content and topic analysis, combined with network analysis, have been used in the past to study longitudinal changes and topics that span various networks. She also called attention to work based heavily in quantitative methods that she asserted could benefit from understanding culture and history. In her own work, she reported, she has been examining methodologies from science technology studies.

Harknett suggested that, instead of thinking about core concepts, it may be more important to consider how to bring members from different fields together. He gave the example of specialists in security studies working more closely with computer scientists. However, he added, organizational research could be used to answer questions about leveraging the expertise of these two disciplines.

An audience member observed that much of what had been discussed during the panel had centered on the spread of ideas across networks, which is somewhat analogous to the way diseases spread. With that analogy in mind, this participant asked whether the panelists thought there might be a way to link epidemiological methods to cyber issues. Lin responded that this is an idea advanced by other researchers, as well as incorporated in models from various disciplines, such as environmental studies. He added that some researchers are actively looking to such disciplines as epidemiology for solutions.

Harknett followed up on Lin's comments by adding that, while models are being drawn from epidemiology and environmental studies, it is important to remember that strategic actors in cyberspace are often purposely attempting to do harm. Viruses and bacteria may hurt us, he added, but they are motivated by survival rather than malicious intent.

Kerr expressed her interest in these analogies. She stated that she is particularly interested in comparison with sustainability from the environmental movement, as well as sustainable business practices. She agreed that Harknett's point about strategic intent is an important one, but suggested that its salience depends on the type of cyber issue being studied.

4

Forecasting Methods and Topics

This panel explored the methods of forecasting through discussion of four topics in which forecasting is particularly important: democratic backsliding, military conflict and violence, epidemics, and environmental security. Suzanne Fry, National Intelligence Council, then commented on these presentations and suggested topics and methodological approaches for future research. The panel closed with an open discussion between the presenters and audience members.

FROM PREDICTION TO PRACTICE: INTEGRATING FORECASTING MODELS INTO PUBLIC HEALTH EDUCATION AND RESPONSE

Kacey Ernst, University of Arizona, focused on the importance of incorporating the social and behavioral sciences into predictive models of vectorborne diseases. She explained that traditional predictive research on such diseases tends to focus on environmental factors, such as temperature, rainfall, and vegetation cover. But while monitoring environmental factors is helpful in identifying baseline risk, she argued, human factors, such as risk behaviors, mobility patterns, and social and political infrastructure, also affect how diseases are transmitted and how those transmissions are detected.

It is well documented, Ernst noted, that temperature and precipitation are drivers of mosquito development. Thus, she said, a basic predictive model using only temperature and precipitation inputs has historically provided accurate predictions of dengue transmission. Researchers have speculated, she continued, that the unexpected peak in dengue transmission experienced during drier years in San Juan, Puerto Rico, occurred at least in part because residents were keeping containers of standing water (an excellent mosquito breeding ground) to water plants.[1] Seeing how this change in human behavior played a role, Ernst and her colleagues began to incorporate demographic factors into model projections. She stressed, however, that demographic factors are not enough; behaviors must also be accounted for in attempting to predict transmission. For example, she explained, the transmission of some vectorborne diseases, such as malaria, is more likely to be predicted by the availability of treatments or behavioral interventions, such as the use of bed nets. For interventions to be effective, she added, it is critical that researchers study the drivers of behavior change.

According to Ernst, social factors are particularly useful when incorporated in early warning systems, which make projections 3–6 months ahead. She explained that early warning systems can be divided into three categories: watch, warning, and emergency. "Watch" systems develop an early assessment of the risk of an emergency event, "warning" systems are used when human disease has been detected, and "emergency" systems come into play when an epidemic or outbreak is under way. Ernst observed that "early warning systems for epidemics face several key challenges, including integration of disparate data streams, changing risk landscapes as new controls, human behavior, and response capacity shift." Thus, she stressed, multiple components must be monitored for early warning system forecasts to be accurate.

As an example of an early warning system, Ernst cited a projection she worked on with colleagues to identify the risk of transmission of the Zika virus in the continental United States.[2] She explained that she and the team, led by Dr. Monaghan at the National Center for Atmospheric Research (NCAR), "incorporated *Aedes aegypti* seasonality, socioeconomic status, travel from endemic countries, and prior dengue infection" to develop accurate predictions of where Zika would most likely be transmitted (see Figure 4-1). She noted that this one-time assessment was developed with the use of climate and travel patterns. However, she argued, systems that process real-time data, such as those used for drought monitoring and early warning of famine, would be better at predicting disease transmission. She

---

[1] Morin, C.W., Monaghan, A.J., Hayden, M.H., Barrera, R., and Ernst, K. (2015) Meteorologically driven simulations of Dengue epidemics in San Juan, PR. *PLOS Neglected Tropical Diseases*, 9(8), e0004002. doi:10.1371/journal.pntd.0004002.

[2] Monaghan, A.J., Morin, C.W., Steinhoff, D.F., Wilhelmi, O., Hayden, M., Quattrochi, D.A., Reiskind, M., Lloyd, A.L., Smith, K., Schmidt, C.A., Scalf, P.E., and Ernst, K. (2016). On the seasonal occurrence and abundance of the Zika virus vector mosquito *Aedes aegypti* in the Contiguous United States. *PLOS Currents*, 8. doi:10.1371/currents.outbreaks.50dfc7f46798675fc63e7d7da563da76.

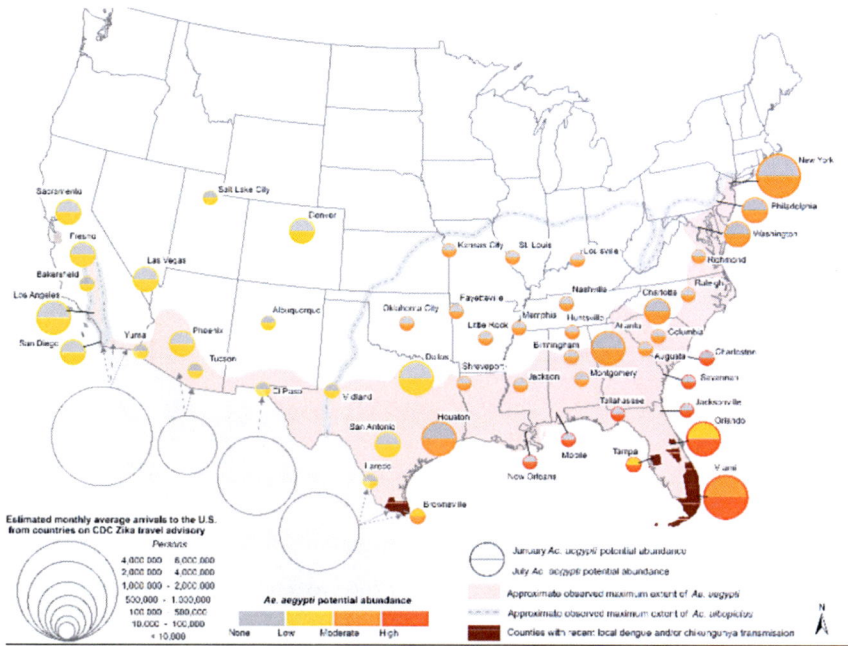

FIGURE 4-1 Early warning map for Zika virus.
SOURCE: Monaghan, A.J., Morin, C.W., Steinhoff, D.F., Wilhelmi, O., Hayden, M., Quattrochi, D.A., Reiskind, M., Lloyd, A.L., Smith, K., Schmidt, C.A., Scalf, P.E., and Ernst, K. (2016). On the seasonal occurrence and abundance of the Zika virus vector mosquito *Aedes aegypti* in the Contiguous United States. *PLOS Currents, 8*. doi:10.1371/currents.outbreaks.50dfc7f46798675fc63e7d7da563da76. Used with permission.

added that early identification can help control an outbreak by making it possible to reduce contact, treat cases quickly to reduce the duration of infectiousness, target interventions, and increase their uptake.

Ernst then pointed to social listening as a potential tool to aid in the early detection of disease outbreaks. By developing algorithms for monitoring keywords across such social media platforms as Twitter, Facebook, and Instagram, and even Internet search engines, she noted, researchers can identify trends in symptoms or illness. However, she cautioned, there are drawbacks to this method. For example, she said, data are often biased by age and geography, and noisy data can make identifying large-scale trends difficult.

Ernst cited community-based participatory surveillance (CBPS) as another method that has shown promise in early detection of disease outbreaks. One example of a successful CBPS system, she noted, is Flu Near You, which has a greater than 90 percent correlation with the Centers for Disease Control and Prevention's influenza surveillance data. She did acknowledge, however, that research is needed to increase participation across demographic groups to reduce bias in the data.

Ernst and her colleagues recently developed a system for symptom monitoring to target mosquito activity and mosquitoborne diseases across regions on the U.S.–Mexico border. To reduce difficulties with recruitment, Ernst plans to leverage Kidenga as a resource. Similar to Flu Near You, Kidenga is an online app that allows members of the community to self-report illness that has been transmitted by mosquito bites. Ernst and her colleagues have been investigating behavior change models with an eye to increasing use of the app. As a result of this research, they have discovered that people are motivated to participate because they consider mosquitoes to be an annoyance, not because they are concerned about the risk of disease.

Ernst closed by suggesting that research is needed to understand how much uncertainty stakeholders are willing to accept before they are willing to invest in early warning systems. Research is also needed, she asserted, to understand what motivates public health partners and the public to take action. She argued further for investment in systems, not just research grants, so that validated early warning systems can be maintained and provide sustainable forecasts.

FORECASTING WATER AVAILABILITY IN ARID REGIONS

Afreen Siddiqi, Massachusetts Institute of Technology and Harvard University, discussed methods of forecasting water availability in arid regions. Because water is essential to human existence, she observed, limited access to water can have a devastating effect on human welfare, societal welfare, and public health.

Siddiqi and her colleagues have been studying countries that are water-stressed. Water is not just a critical resource, Siddiqi explained, but also a finite one. Thus, she said, no additional water supply is available to accommodate an increase in population; when a population increases, the amount of water per capita decreases. Figure 4-2 shows the decrease in per capita water supply in water-stressed regions. Siddiqi pointed out that the red line at the top of the figure represents the water poverty line defined by the United Nations. Thus it is clear that many of these countries are already in an extreme situation.

Siddiqi emphasized that solving the problem of water scarcity requires

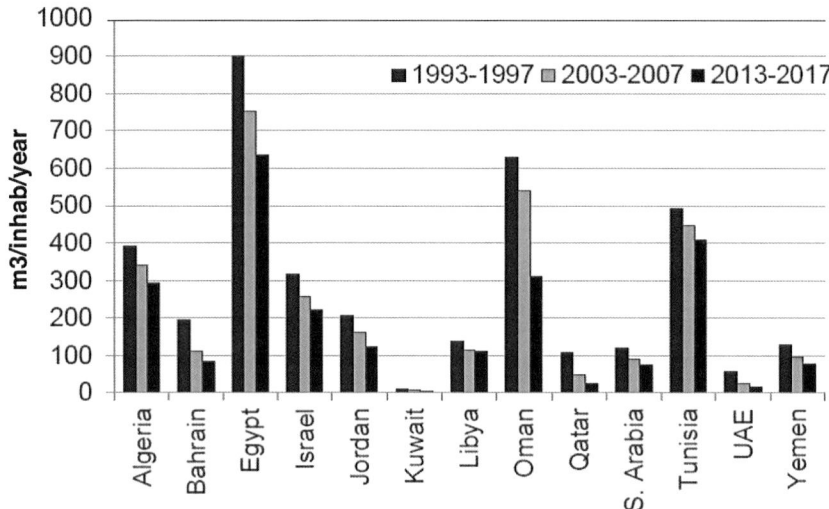

FIGURE 4-2 Per capita water supply in water-stressed regions.
SOURCE: Food and Agriculture Organization of the United Nations. (2016). *AQUASTAT* database. Available: http://www.fao.org/nr/water/aquastat/data/query/index.html?lang=en [April 2018].

examining what the future may look like years in advance because any investment made now must be sustainable in the long term, and also must consider infrastructures that rely on water, such as energy and agriculture. Because experience has shown that water forecasting methods using historical data are not helpful, she and her colleagues initiated a research program to find a method that would work. They began by identifying large-scale infrastructure projects under consideration in arid regions. Next, Siddiqi explained, she and her colleagues assessed the likelihood of these projects being implemented and how much water they could be expected to add to the system.

When considering the likelihood of implementation, Siddiqi and her colleagues studied regional decision makers and identified the factors likely to be significant in their decision-making process. They then used multi-criteria decision analysis methods to organize and code the collected data. According to Siddiqi, it was also necessary to identify several key assumptions:

- The resource is being developed through a discrete set of infrastructure projects.

- The resource is being developed for direct use and cannot be substituted for through trade and imports.
- The decisions are being made by a specific group of key actors.
- The decision makers are evaluating each project using a discrete set of factors.

The research team then organized the various projects and evaluated them based on the decision criteria, Siddiqi continued. These data were then placed in a performance matrix, and the projects were compared. Siddiqi explained that the next step was to compare the results of the team's analysis with information about past projects known to have been commissioned and implemented. Finally, the team assessed the likelihood of future project selection by evaluating performance on different preference sets and conducted an evaluation in which the probabilities of importance for different criteria were varied. Once they had decided that a project was likely to be implemented, Siddiqi explained, they assessed the amount of water the project would be expected to add to the system.

As an example, Siddiqi shared results of the team's methodology after it had been applied to identifying projects in Jordan.[3] She noted that the projects being evaluated ranged in size and scope: some were large desalination projects, while others were smaller wastewater treatment projects. She pointed out that desalination systems, which remove salt from seawater so that it is safe for human consumption, are widely employed in countries where water is scarce.

According to Siddiqi, decision makers use a least-cost approach on large infrastructure projects, meaning that they often start with the least expensive system and move on to other systems from there. She explained that she and her colleagues began by developing a detailed analysis of the stakeholders involved in project selection. They then held structured interviews with these stakeholders to understand their decision-making process. Table 4-1 shows the decision criteria and their ranking as provided by the decision makers.

Reviewing the decision criteria in Table 4-1, Siddiqi noted that, because many of the large-scale infrastructure projects in Jordan are financed by foreign financiers, foreign investment potential is a significant consideration for stakeholders. She observed that political feasibility is another important factor for decision makers. She pointed out that, because of the sociopolitical aspects of many water infrastructure projects and the resulting

---

[3] Siddiqi, A., Ereiqat, F., and Anadon, L.D. (2016). Formulating expectations for future water availability through infrastructure development decisions in arid regions. *Systems Engineering, 19*(2), 101–110.

TABLE 4-1 Decision Criteria and Their Ranking as Provided by Decision Makers in Jordan

	Decision Maker 1[a]	Decision Maker 2[a]	Decision Maker 3[b]	Decision Maker 4[c]	Decision Maker 5[c]
1	Societal Demand	Cost / Annual Supply	Political Feasibility	Cost	Cost
2	Cost	Sectoral Priorities	Cost	Foreign Investment Potential	Foreign Investment Potential
3	Political Feasibility	Geographic Distribution	Annual Supply	Annual Supply	Annual Supply
4	Foreign Investment Potential	Environmental Impact	Environmental Impact	Political Feasibility	Political Feasibility
5		Resource Sustainability	Foreign Investment Potential	Social Priority	Social Priority
6			Socioeconomic Development	Environmental Impact	Harmful Environmental Impacts
7				Supply Sustainability	Supply Sustainability

[a]Ministry of Water and Irrigation
[b]Ministry of Planning and International Cooperation
[c]Ministry of Environment

SOURCE: Adapted from Siddiqi, A., Ereiqat, F., and Anadon, L.D. (2016). Formulating expectations for future water availability through infrastructure development decisions in arid regions. *Systems Engineering*, 19(2), 101–110. Used with permission.

political implications, it can be difficult for such projects to be approved for development.

After performing their initial analysis, Siddiqi and her colleagues determined that the Waste Water Treatment Expansion (WWTE) project had an 83 percent chance of being implemented. They then considered which project would most likely be implemented if WWTE were taken out of the equation. From that analysis, they predicted that the Disi Pipeline would be next in line for implementation.

Siddiqi and her colleagues also considered scenarios in which it was possible that a dominant decision maker set the priorities for water projects. This analysis gave them a chance to see how changing priorities affected the outcomes.

Siddiqi closed by delineating a few of the limitations of this study. First, she noted that, although her team's method successfully predicted the outcome of interest, it should not be assumed that the team has developed a unique set of predictive factors. She added that it is not always easy to identify the decision makers involved or their priorities. Furthermore, decision makers' priorities in a country may change because of changes occurring internationally or within the country.

AUTHORITARIAN BACKSLIDING: DRIVERS, TRENDS, AND IMPLICATIONS

Jennifer Dresden, Georgetown University, focused on the measurement and forecasting of what is termed "authoritarian backsliding," also called in the literature "democratic backsliding," "democratic reversal," "autocratization," and "democratic deconsolidation." Authoritarian backsliding, she explained, refers to "actions taken by government or state actors to degrade democratic institutions and procedures that impart horizontal or vertical constraints on government power." She added that "the imparting of constraints refers to the institutions and the procedures, not the backsliding itself. Backsliding is the removal of constraints on power, typically by the executive."

Dresden explained further that use of the term "democratic" does not necessarily mean a country is already democratic. Many democratic institutions exist (e.g., elections, political parties), she observed, but not many democracies in practice. However, she elaborated, backsliding can happen in full democracies—a phenomenon that has been on the rise since 2014—as well as in hybrid regimes. She clarified that the latter regimes may appear democratic in that they usually have democratic institutions, such as elections, but they are also likely to have elements found in authoritarian regimes. She cited Turkey as an example of a country that had been moving toward becoming a democracy but has been backsliding in recent years.

Although backsliding is not new, Dresden explained, it began to gain attention from the policy community only in 2007 after the failure of the color revolutions (a collection of nonviolent uprisings in the 2000s). However, she asserted, the phenomenon is important to international security in two ways. First, she said, "many of the international institutions that we think of as being stabilizing in the international community, like NATO and the European Union, for example, have as part of their core foundation an expectation that there will be adherence to a certain set of democratic norms and practices. When those start to erode, you start to see countries getting a little uncomfortable with one another." For example, she suggested, recent backsliding in Hungary and Poland has caused some to question the stability of these countries. She added that security may also be compromised when backsliding encourages citizens to flee their country, sometimes without formally applying for asylum, as is happening in Venezuela.

Backsliding, Dresden continued, tends to come in three different forms: coups d'état (the overthrow of executive powers by security forces), expansion of executive power (by removing term limits or making changes to the legal structure), and electoral manipulation (which can include the jailing of opposition leaders). However, she noted, consensus is lacking on what causes backsliding to happen, and existing research on this question using forecasting models is not directly relevant to current circumstances. She suggested that part of the problem may be that researchers have "measure[ed] backslides in terms of the collapse of a government regime" but that backsliding is not always that clear-cut: it may also be a relevant way to analyze gray areas in terms of what can be considered democratic.

Table 4-2 shows a matrix developed by Dresden, designed to clarify various causes of backsliding identified in prior studies. There is some agreement, she explained, on backsliding that falls in the structural/institutional category. "The higher-quality democracy you have, the stronger your institutions are," she observed, "the less likely you are to experience backsliding." One risk factor on which researchers do agree as significant, she pointed out, is polarized political competition. Referring to the presentations on the strategic use of information summarized in Chapter 3, she noted that polarization is a method often employed in cyberwarfare.

According to Dresden, the literature often suggests that democracies are especially vulnerable to backsliding in the months leading up to an election. She argued, however, that this view probably is no longer accurate given that researchers are beginning to see backsliding behavior begin well before an election is scheduled. She noted that backsliding strategies are often used when incumbents worry that their position in the current system is no longer secure. To protect their status, these incumbents may take steps—such as eliminating term limits—to maintain their position in the future.

TABLE 4-2 Factors That Increase or Decrease the Risk of Authoritarian Backsliding

	Risk Increasing	Risk Reducing
STRUCTURAL/ INSTITUTIONAL	Demographic considerations	Robust civil liberties
	Poverty	Institutional form
	Economic inequality	Wealth
	Weak institutions	International linkage/leverage
	Regime "adolescence"	
AGENT-CENTRIC	Polarized political competition	High margins of victory in free and fair elections
	Violent acts by opposition	Opposition-inclusive government
	International "autocracy promotion" (maybe)	

SOURCE: Adapted from Jennifer Dresden presentation at workshop.

Dresden closed with a few final thoughts on backsliding. First, she observed that most forms of backsliding are not as dramatic and abrupt as one might expect. Backsliding is often a collection of a series of subtle actions that slowly erode democracy. Furthermore, she noted, "the background conditions that put a country at risk [of backsliding] are not the same as the proximate conditions that trigger it." "Institutional weakness can persist for a very long time before the opposition actually becomes threatening and motivates a response from the incumbent," she elaborated. She also argued that more research is needed to understand what motivates an incumbent to use one strategy over another in a given situation. Finally, she said, because backsliding is often reactive, the "interaction between the incumbent and opposition actors is central to backsliding processes."

CONNECTING THEORY TO POLICY WITH FORECASTING

According to Christopher Gelpi, Ohio State University, quantitative research in international relations is often dismissed as not being policy-relevant. In his presentation, he challenged this assumption by arguing that some forecasting methods can actually bridge theory and policy.

Gelpi began by identifying two ways in which researchers attempt to make policy-relevant predictions. The first is the traditional method of collecting data, examining the data using statistical analysis, and then making a prediction based on that analysis. The second method, according to Gelpi, is to use forecasting models, three types of which are frequently used in the fields of international relations and comparative politics: game theoretic models, which study interactions between decision makers in competitive situations; time series models, which involve the coding and analysis of event data over a period of time; and structural models, which make a prediction by using an estimated set of coefficients to measure data that have been collected on a set of covariates. Gelpi asserted that structural models are the best method for connecting theory and policy because—unlike game theoretic and time series models—they are both theoretical and generalizable.

According to Gelpi, another good method for bridging theory and policy is the random forest model. Using the prediction of civil wars as an example, he explained that the random forest model takes the variables provided by researchers and uses an algorithm to divide that dataset into "civil war" and "not civil war" cases.[4] Gelpi explained that, because the random forest model yields a relatively small number of false positives, it is a good choice for providing a policy-relevant forecast.

According to Gelpi, several methodological challenges can be addressed with the use of forecasting methods. The first such challenge he identified was "overfitting or making models excessively complex." For example, he explained, if a researcher applies a theory against a set of cases, such as alliances in the Cold War era, but the theory does not work, applying a new theory to predict the same cases can make it difficult to know whether the researcher is "crafting an explanation that generalizes" or "just overfitting the model to the data that we happen to observe."

Another challenge Gelpi has observed is that both quantitative and qualitative researchers will often overgeneralize models. For example, he noted, a quantitative scholar may "run an analysis on data from the Cold War and say democracy is correlated with peace," and then, based on that information, make "a very general claim [that] democracy causes peace across all space and time," which likely cannot be supported by the data.

Gelpi has also found that researchers will choose theories with effects that are statistically significant, but it is unclear which effects are substantively significant. This may occur if a researcher has generated marginal effects from models in which all variables but one have been held constant. However, this is not realistic, Gelpi argued. "It's like imagining an

---

[4] Muchlinski, D., Siroky, D., He, J., and Kocher, M. (2015). Comparing random forest with logistic regression for predicting class-imbalanced civil war onset data. *Political Analysis*, 24(1), 87–103.

authoritarian Canada or something like that," he said. "You imagine what Canada's foreign policy would be like if they were authoritarian. Authoritarian Canada is not a thing. There's a whole combination of other things that are correlated with a democracy."

To demonstrate how forecasting can help correct overgeneralization, Gelpi shared the results of a study he recently conducted with a former graduate student.[5] Figure 4-3 depicts a model of military conflict over a period of time. Gelpi explained that he and his colleague "found that there were different eras of international politics where the causal model of war was really different." In Figure 4-3, Gelpi noted, the receiver operating characteristic (ROC) curves and the x-axis are flipped so that the scale can be read to show that "the vertical axis is the true-positive rate and the horizontal axis is the false-positive rate." He added that the bottom line represents both forecasts "trying to predict militarized disputes in the Cold War era." The top model, he continued, which has been calibrated based on Cold War–era data, has a strong ROC curve (the top line curved toward the upper left), whereas the bottom model, which was calibrated "on the interwar period and then forecasted onto the Cold War period," has a much weaker ROC curve, indicating that this model is a much weaker fit.

Gelpi then shared results of a study he conducted to forecast transnational terrorism.[6] One finding of this study, he reported, was "that democratic states are likely to be targets of terrorism" (see Figure 4-4). He and a colleague then carried out a forecasting analysis to "see how much… including or excluding democracy from our forecasting model actually changes our ability to forecast terrorist attacks." According to Gelpi, they found that democracy as a variable contributed very little to their model's ability to predict terrorist attacks.

Gelpi closed by reiterating that structural models can be a useful tool in making policy-relevant predictions. However, he stressed, structural models should not be used to identify a causal connection; rather, the forecasting models described in his presentation should be supplemented with a causal inference model, such as statistical matching.

---

[5] Jenke, L., and Gelpi, C. (2016). Theme and variations: Historical contingencies in the causal model of inter-state conflict. *Journal of Conflict Resolution*, 61(10), 2262–2284. doi:10.1177/0022002715615190.

[6] Gelpi, C., and Avdan. N. (2015). Democracies at risk? A forecasting analysis of regime type and the risk of terrorist attack. *Conflict Management and Peace Science*, 35(1), 18–42.

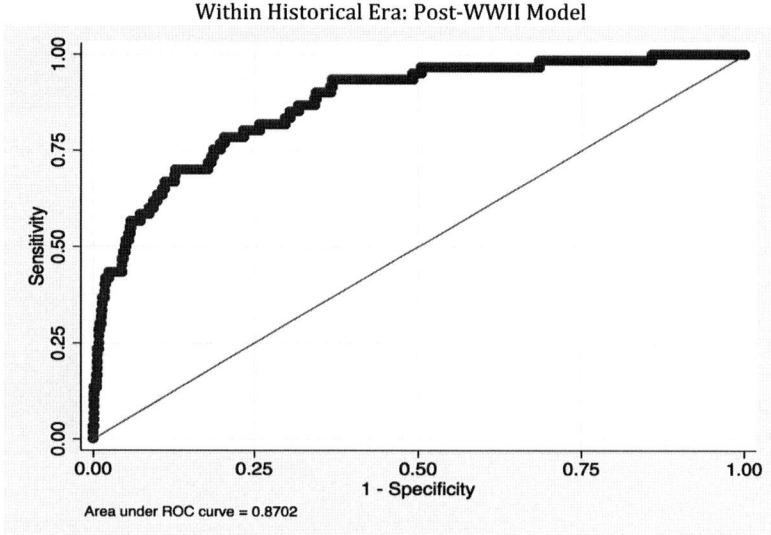
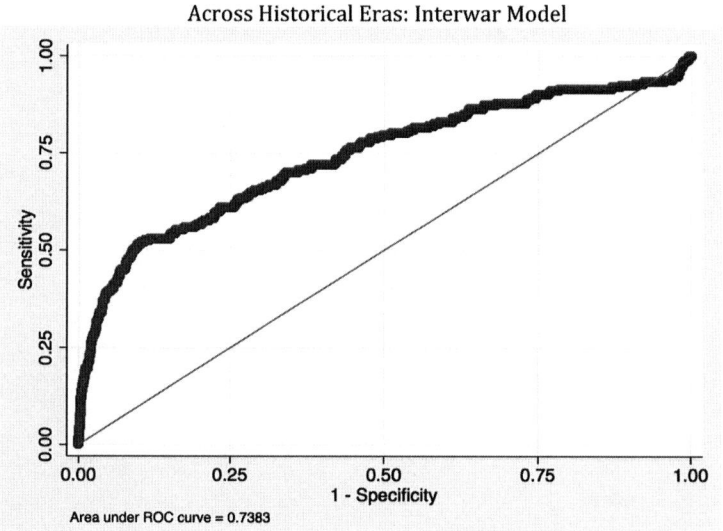

FIGURE 4-3 Overgeneralization of effects.
SOURCE: Jenke, L., and Gelpi, C. (2016). Theme and variations: Historical contingencies in the causal model of inter-state conflict. *Journal of Conflict Resolution*, 61(10), 2262–2284. doi:10.1177/0022002715615190. Reprinted with permission.

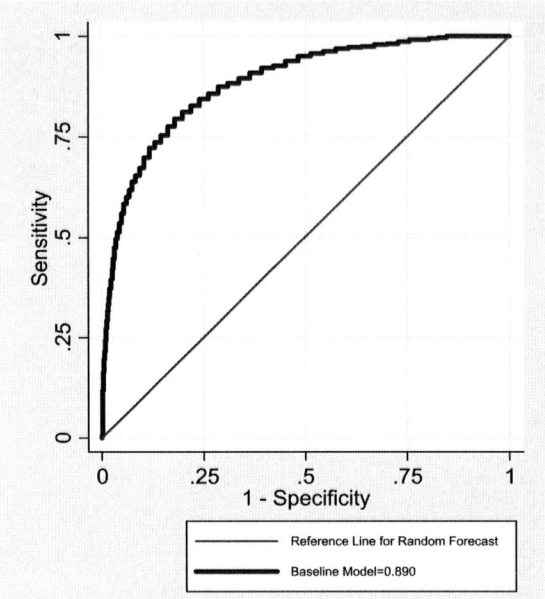

FIGURE 4-4 Democracy and terrorism, transnational terrorist attacks.
SOURCE: Gelpi, C., and Avdan. N. (2015). Democracies at risk? A forecasting analysis of regime type and the risk of terrorist attack. *Conflict Management and Peace Science*, 35(1), 18–42. Reprinted with permission.

REMARKS FROM SUZANNE FRY

Fry began by stating that the Intelligence Community (IC) values and utilizes forecasts from both the natural and the social sciences. However, she said, only a small portion of the analytic community understands how to use them. She pointed out that the majority of the IC's customers are policy makers, who are more comfortable making decisions when quantitative data are translated into a narrative. She emphasized the importance of Gelpi's discussion of connecting forecasting with theory, because if an analysis begins with a well-developed theory, the analyst will find it easier to communicate the information in narrative form.

According to Fry, it would also be helpful if analysts were given guidance as to when history is no longer a helpful guide. Advances in technology, for example, may cause historical data to be irrelevant in some situations, she argued.

Fry added that disciplinary boundaries can also create forecasting challenges. Scholars in comparative politics and international relations often have limited knowledge of theories and methodologies outside of their area of expertise, she noted, suggesting that it would be beneficial if scholars could overcome these limitations.

Fry also suggested three types of data that she believes should be represented more commonly in forecasting models. The first is demographic data. According to Fry, much of what is known about political behavior is based on demographic data. Furthermore, she asserted, it is important for the IC to maintain access to a variety of demographic data. Equally important, she suggested, are data on subnational structural phenomena and the associated behavioral phenomena. Finally, she highlighted systematic data on policy treatments as important to include in forecasting models. Such data are often not available when needed, she argued, hampering an analyst's ability to provide timely information.

According to Fry, detecting changes in the balance of power or influence of major powers internationally is a topic of particular interest to the IC. She added that identifying core systemic risks in the international community could also be useful to the IC. Systemic risk analysis is a well-developed methodology in the natural sciences, she observed, but is not applied as often as it could be in the social sciences.

Turning to regime types, Fry asserted that, in addition to hybrid regimes, administrative capacity—whether things are improving or deteriorating—is another dimension of governance that requires more research. Moreover, "when you think about outcomes of interest to forecast," she suggested, "make sure that you scrub them for the types of political or ideological biases they might be containing because we want to make sure that these tools are useful over time."

Fry closed by responding to Ernst's question about what motivates the IC to act upon warning statements and forecasts. She explained that one of the most important factors in motivating action is the ability to explain a forecast. To give an example, she noted that when the Ebola crisis occurred the IC was flooded with forecasts anticipating incredibly high death tolls, but analysts were so inundated with these reports that they began not to take them seriously. In such a situation, Fry suggested, it would be helpful if forecasts were provided with interpretive guidance that clearly explains the research design and data analyzed.

DISCUSSION

Addressing all panelists, a participant opened the discussion session by asking them to provide their thoughts on "the mix of strong or weak theory and mix of inductive or deductive elements" in forecasting with respect to their discipline.

Ernst responded that when thinking in terms of theoretical models it is helpful to have an initial layer that is rooted in biological processes, which provides well-established parameters that dictate the baseline risk. However, she suggested, epidemiologists have not done a great job of incorporating elements from the social sciences. She said that while listening to the panel presentations she began to realize just how relevant public health and the sociopolitical sciences are to one another; for example, an epidemic could be a factor pushing a state to the point of instability. She argued that more work is needed to develop a theoretical model that reflects this connection between pandemics and political stability.

Siddiqi noted that much of the work discussed in her presentation related to decision analysis. Decision analysis, she said, is rooted in the assumption that options are being reviewed and weighed by rational and logical decision makers. Looking at cases in this way, she suggested, is a rather simple approach to developing simulations that provide a number of future possibilities. She also pointed out that decision analysis is well established, theoretical, and practical.

Dresden asserted that theory is crucial to understanding backsliding. She stated that such questions as What are the areas we should be paying attention to? and What changes would meaningfully degrade the accountability in a system? are theoretically driven. She also pointed out that theoretical considerations are relevant to answering questions about the strategic interactions between incumbents and opposition groups. Finally, she suggested that inductive work is needed to increase the accuracy of models so they can be used to consider such questions as Who counts as the opposition? and What is the set of possible actions or strategies or tactics in any given context?

Gelpi suggested that international relations theory is strongest in the middle range, which involves examining well-established theories on such questions as how democracy and trade affect the likelihood that force will be used. However, he added, more work is needed on how to integrate these questions. He asserted that linearity is often imposed when it should not be, and that "the random forest model is good because it does not impose linearity." Gelpi also suggested that more work is needed on scope conditions. "I think we have a bunch of tools that we can apply where we know these things are associated with violence in various ways," he said, "but exactly how they fit together I think is weaker."

Another participant asked whether the IC agrees with the view that predictions are better if they are cast in specific quantitative terms. Fry responded by pointing out that not all people think in terms of numbers and probabilities. Furthermore, she observed, predicted percentages are often presented using such estimative phrases as "roughly 10 percent" or "70 percent likelihood." To understand what these numbers mean, it is important that the IC have access to two different types of forecasters to aid in the decision-making process: individuals with deep expertise in a specific area and people that know "a lot about lots of different things." She added that, although deep country experts or deep functional experts may work with many different models, "they tend to be variants on one phenomenon." On the other hand, she continued, those that know "a lot about lots of different things" are often very good at forecasting because they have access to a variety of models that allow them to "think about different ways of envisioning an outcome." It is also important, she stressed, to know which type of forecaster is needed in a given situation.

Gelpi added that quantitative models are helpful because they force people to "be specific and concrete" in defining the variables and measurements being used. He also seconded Fry's comments, and suggested that scholars need to be careful about being so committed to a particular set of theories that they become unwilling to change or develop other methods.

5

Trends in Social Science Methods

Andrew Bennett, Georgetown University, presented a broad overview of social science methods relevant to the Intelligence Community (IC). He began by noting two countervailing trends in these methods.

First, Bennett highlighted the replication crisis—the inability to reproduce published scientific findings—as a trend that has affected disciplines across the social, physical, and medical sciences. This bias, he suggested, is likely due to such bad practices as p-hacking, or mining data to uncover statistically significant results not included in the original study hypothesis, and publication bias, or only publishing statistically significant findings. As a countermeasure to publication bias, he noted, journals have started preregistering experimental trials.

Countering publication bias, however, are methodological advances in the social sciences, Bennett asserted. He cited big data, computer-assisted content analysis, machine learning, agent-based modeling (ABM), natural experiments, group-based superforecasting, new methods in case studies, and multimethods research as examples of emerging tools and methods benefiting the social sciences.

Discussing such technological advances as big data, computer-assisted content analysis, and machine learning, Bennett observed that big data has changed research practices in a number of ways. First, he said, researchers now have access to a growing amount of real-time and more fine-grained data from a variety of sources, such as social media activities, event data, and geographic information systems. He gave the example of satellite images, such as those recently taken of burning villages in Myanmar, which

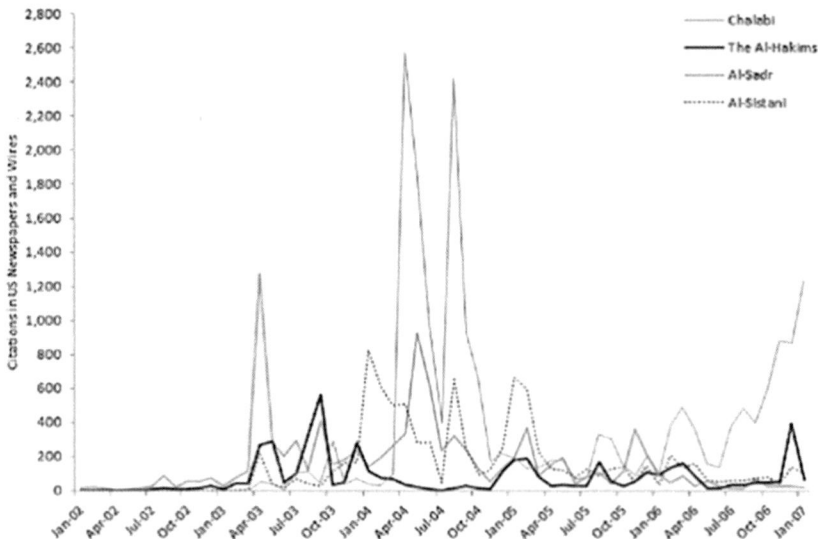

FIGURE 5-1 Media mentions of Iraqi leaders, January 2002–January 2007.
SOURCE: Sargsyan, I., and Bennett, A. (2016). Discursive emotional appeals in sustaining violent social movements in Iraq, 2003–2011. *Security Studies*, 25(4), 630. Reprinted with permission.

allow researchers, policy makers, and other government officials to monitor events across the globe.

Bennett then turned to computer-assisted content analysis, which, he observed, has increased in both speed and accuracy as a result of improved models of syntax and natural language processing. He noted that researchers have further benefited from advances in audio and visual data processing. However, he cautioned, these advances also give people the ability to create false audio and video clips, similar to the recent Obama lip syncing video,[1] helping to make fake news appear more convincing.

Bennett shared the results of a study he conducted with one of his students to show how even something as simple as word counts can provide revealing insights (see Figure 5-1). By tracking media mentions for Iraqi leaders, Bennett and his student could identify when the influence of politi-

---

[1] Suwajanakorn, S., Seitz, S.M., and Kemelmacher-Shlizerman, I. (2017). Synthesizing Obama: Learning lip sync from audio. *ACM Transactions on Graphics, 36*(4, Art. 95), 1–13. Available: https://grail.cs.washington.edu/projects/AudioToObama/siggraph17_obama.pdf [January 2018].

cal leaders was rising and falling. As an example, he pointed to Figure 5-1, which shows a sudden jump in mentions for Muqtada Al-Sadr around 2004, suggesting that he went undetected until it became obvious that he was a key figure in the Iraqi leadership.

Bennett continued by highlighting significant advances in machine learning. As Christopher Gelpi had discussed in his presentation on forecasting military conflict and violence (see Chapter 4), the random forest approach is one example of a machine learning technique that has improved the predictive power of logistic regression. However, Bennett suggested, random forest and other machine learning techniques have their limitations. As an example, he cited the need for a significant amount of data for machine learning models to be effective. Furthermore, he observed, while machine learning techniques are helpful tools when a researcher is attempting to predict events, they do not help explain why an event occurred. Another limitation, he added, is that machine learning models have the ability to analyze only historical data.

Bennett identified ABM as another useful computational tool. Using ABM, he explained, researchers can test theories about behavior by simulating how an actor or group of actors might behave in a specific situation or environment. To illustrate, he noted that, by entering population data, geographic checkpoints, and other relevant data, ABM allows researchers to predict outcomes related to specific events, such as where refugees may flee during an outbreak of violence.

Bennett also pointed to a resurgence of interest in experiments, particularly natural experiments. The reason for this resurgence, he suggested, is that experiments, including natural experiments, are more accurate than other methods in identifying causal connections. However, he observed, the IC may want to proceed with caution when planning experiments of their own, and in some cases, it may be more appropriate for them to encourage or sponsor experimental research.

Turning to group-based superforecasting, Bennett described the Good Judgment Project, a 5-year government-funded study of the use of crowdsourcing to improve the accuracy of forecasting world events. He explained that this project is relevant because it has demonstrated that, with training, group forecasters (superforecasters) are more accurate than individual forecasters at predicting events. Currently, group superforecastering methods achieve 80–85 percent accuracy, whereas an individual forecaster is able to achieve 50–60 percent accuracy. Although it is hoped that the project will improve prediction accuracy by coupling human analysis with computer algorithms, Bennett suggested that research should also be initiated to identify the best methods for training superforecasters. Furthermore, he observed, research incorporating Bayesian analysis might be useful in improving accuracy.

Bennett next reported that he is currently working on two new case study methods: Bayesian process tracing and typological theorizing. He explained that process tracing is much like detective work: it involves identifying "suspects" (alternative explanations) and examining "clues" (evidence) to determine what caused the outcome of the case being studied. Bennett and his colleagues, however, have initiated research to assess the usefulness of explicit Bayesian process tracing. According to Bennett, the 2003 assessment that Iraq possessed weapons of mass destruction would likely have been dismissed if the forecasters had used explicit Bayesian analysis. This is because, he elaborated, even if Iraq's aluminum tubes were meant to be used in a nuclear weapons program, the nonexistence of evidence on the many other components that would have been necessary for a nuclear program would have been a strong indication that Iraq did not have such a program. However, he suggested that more research is needed to confirm whether explicit Bayesian process tracing improves explanations and predictions.

Bennett then introduced the second new case study method, typological theorizing, which involves "trying to theorize about how different mechanisms and variables interact in different combinations." He explained that cases are categorized as either theoretical types or combinations of variables to address "high-order interaction effects." In process tracing, typological theorizing can help with case selection, he noted. He described the method as similar to statistical matching, except that it uses "coarsened exact matching" to identify good analogies for current policy cases and cast doubt on bad historical analogies to current events.

Finally, Bennett elaborated on multimethods research—the combined use of quantitative and qualitative methods—as another major trend in the social sciences. The combination of these methods, he explained, allows researchers to analyze both population-wide and individual patterns. Furthermore, he suggested, multimethods research may be especially helpful in reducing the number of false positives in the forecasting of rare events.

Bennett closed by suggesting that both academia and the IC consider combining methods when possible. In his view, a best practice would be to combine machine learning, group forecasting, and automated real-time data collection. Moreover, he believes that case studies should be used to identify holes in the data collection and explain outlier cases, or cases that do not have the predicted outcomes. Doing so, he argued, can help identify variables that were omitted from the quantitative models that produced the wrong predictions on the outlier cases.

6

Closing Thoughts

The workshop closed with an opportunity for reflection and discussion led by three scholars who had been asked to listen throughout the day and offer their observations—Jim Goldgeier, American University; William Thompson, Indiana University; and Sean Lynn-Jones, Harvard University. Moderator Andrew Bennett, Georgetown University, opened the discussion by asking the three for their thoughts about high-priority topics that had not been raised in the presentations and ensuing discussion, and the discussion then turned to general reflections on workshop themes.

MISSING TOPICS

Goldgeier pointed to an approach that had not been mentioned: the use of comparative scenario analysis as a method for generating policy-relevant research questions. He identified this as a way to think about "plausible alternative futures 5 years down the road." By identifying common patterns within those scenarios, he suggested, one can discern potentially significant developments or trends that may drive international politics. He cited workshops sponsored by the Bridging the Gap project[1] as an example of how researchers develop scenarios for this purpose.

To illustrate the value of this approach, Goldgeier noted that he and his colleagues had developed in 2006 a scenario of a global financial crisis that started in the U.S. housing and banking sectors. He explained that, in a scenario they developed for 2009, "an event in the Middle East leads to

---

[1] For more information, see http://bridgingthegapproject.org [December 2017].

instability in a regime that then creates instability across the region and efforts to democratize." Such scenarios are not designed to make predictions, he cautioned, and indeed when they are used in that way, they may distract from deeper thinking about policy-relevant research questions. He believes that, although this approach is seldom used in political science, it can be particularly useful to the Intelligence Community.

Lynn-Jones began by observing that the topics covered in the workshop were "very much cutting-edge" and did not include many topics that might have been expected based on a review of the most-read articles in *International Security*. As examples of the latter topics, he cited nuclear proliferation and deterrence; major conventional conflict, such as with China; and terrorism. Nuclear proliferation, for instance, has recently been what he termed "a reviving area of research," in which researchers have been offering new explanations for the phenomenon and suggesting ways to limit it in a "post-unipolar world."

Another important topic not addressed in the workshop presentations, Lynn-Jones suggested, was the study of insurgent and military groups. Interesting recent research, he noted, has examined "what makes them tick, why they fragment, why they don't fragment, why some like ISIS seem to come out of nowhere and become very major players." Conducting this kind of research is difficult, he added, and such work as interviewing ISIS fighters is quite dangerous.

Focusing on the future, Thompson pointed to some very long term issues not mentioned at the workshop. With reference to Afreen Siddiqi's presentation on forecasting water scarcity, for example, Thompson suggested that scarcity of food and energy will also be a growing problem as the effects of global warming continue to be felt. He suggested that these shortages will likely cause the most significant problems in areas near the equator and in arid regions, and some areas may run completely out of water and food. Epidemics are another source of disruption that can be foreseen, he noted. He observed that somewhat regular patterns of frequency can be seen in the recurrence of the most serious pandemics if one looks across millennia, and it is reasonable to expect another pandemic of the type that can cause "major die-offs of populations."

Thompson also pointed to ethnic conflicts. Study of these conflicts has been hampered in the past, he asserted, by imperfect data that appeared to "suggest that ethnicity didn't have anything to do with civil wars." He noted, however, that more recent work focused on political discrimination has produced important advances in this area.

Finally, Thompson identified escalation of conflict as another topic on which work is needed. The structure of escalation is well documented, he said: "We know who goes to war, who wins wars, [and] who loses wars," but "we don't understand what happens on the crisis battlefield" that changes a dispute into a more serious conflict.

Thompson closed with thoughts about the changing role of the United States on the world stage. Researchers in global trends, he noted, have moved toward defining the U.S. foreign policy role as "first among equals" rather than as world leader, but they have not fully explored the potential effects of a scenario in which the United States is no longer "first" and the world lacks a leader. Since 1815, Thompson argued, Great Britain and the United States have provided "governance and leadership," which may have been intermittent and not always beneficial, but they have been a source of global stability. If the Chinese do not step into the role of world leader, he suggested, the result will be "a more region-oriented world as opposed to the global world" that has been the status quo. Such a development, he believes, would have implications for most international issues, but has not been adequately studied.

WORKSHOP THEMES

Goldgeier identified several themes he had noted across the workshop presentations. The first was that domestic and international issues can no longer be adequately studied as separate topics. "Foreign policy actions are often the result of the domestic political needs of leaders," Goldgeier asserted, and the way power is distributed across different types of actors has been changing. He suggested that these points have been known, but that researchers have not fully acknowledged their implications. For example, he said, the discussion of nonstate actors (see Chapter 2) had demonstrated that new terminology is needed to take into account the growing role of cyberpower and the changing roles and behaviors of different types of actors. Thus, he suggested, the workshop discussions had showed that thinking in terms of "an international system dominated by great powers defined in traditional power terms and focusing on great power competition" is too limiting.

"The answers will not come from any single discipline," Goldgeier continued. The need for interdisciplinary work and new conceptual tools has long been known, he observed, but is not yet fully reflected in current research. Political science has often drawn concepts from other disciplines, he noted, and today there is a heightened need for such interactions. He faulted two institutions for the problem. First, he observed, foundations played a major role in engaging political scientists and physicists to collaborate in addressing the risks of nuclear war during the Cold War years. They have been much slower, in his view, to sponsor the collaborations, such as between social scientists and computer or climate scientists, needed to address current problems. Goldgeier also faulted university programs in international policy for not doing enough to bring together researchers from different disciplines to address pressing questions.

Goldgeier closed with the observation that a significant challenge in the study of policy is a "failure of imagination." It was no secret, he observed, that the breakup of the Soviet Union and the end of the Cold War meant a significant loss of status for the leadership of the Russian state and its leaders. President Bill Clinton, he said, pushed for Russia to be included in the Group of Eight (G8) in part because he recognized that the Russian leader, Boris Yeltsin, needed a sign of status to compensate for the comparative strengthening of NATO. What researchers have not explored adequately, in Goldgeier's view, is whether more concrete support for Yeltsin's governance might have had beneficial effects in subsequent years. Similarly, he observed, the decision of other powers to wage war in Kosovo and Iraq without the authorization of the United Nations Security Council because of Russia's expected veto undermined Russia's perception of the value of its membership in that body. Thus, he suggested, it might have been expected that Russia would seek other ways to undermine other powers.

Goldgeier went on to say that, even when developments are expected, it can be difficult to consider the interconnections among elements of an international situation in a way that supports an effective policy response. It was well known, for example, that "the Russians wanted to be seen as equals," he observed, but treating them as equals would have interfered with other policies the United States was pursuing.

Lynn-Jones began with some observations about the study of status. First, he pointed to the role of emotion in explaining why status matters and how it influences domestic political debates. "Disruptive influence operations succeed not when they make rational arguments," he suggested, "but when they appeal to emotions, and people are persuaded to believe something and will not change that belief even though it is not true."

Lynn-Jones also highlighted the importance of considering whether the study of status yields findings different from those that would emerge from the study of other variables, such as the pursuit of power, wealth, national interest, or security. Work on status, he noted, has applied such concepts as social identity theory (see Chapter 2) to international relations. He suggested that including other variables in the analysis might yield policy approaches that would produce better outcomes. "Awareness of status certainly factored into U.S. policy toward Russia after the collapse of the Soviet Union," he observed, but the resulting U.S. policies may not have been optimal. "It seems," he suggested, that "the basic policy lesson comes out of this that you don't want to make a state feel that it is being deprived of its status. Exercise restraint in various ways unless you can somehow dupe a state into believing that it can accept a lesser role and be satisfied with a new form of status."

The issues of cybersecurity and information warfare call for very different strategic uses of information, in Lynn-Jones's view, because analysis of these issues generally begins with problems, such as the decline of Internet freedom in Russia or the threat to American institutions and political processes posed by information warfare. Unfortunately, he asserted, the conceptual apparatus for addressing these problems is not well developed. "We don't have a concept in search of a problem to solve," he said; "we have a problem that is still looking for concepts." Traditional analysis of deterrence, he added, is based on a dichotomy between peace and war, so that "if you want to keep the peace, you threaten some form of retaliation as soon as the other party engages in unacceptable behavior." He suggested that this dichotomy is not relevant in the cyber world because it is the locus of continuous warfare operations. Lasting deterrent mechanisms are not available, he observed.

Lynn-Jones also said he was struck by the importance of the power of nonstate actors, although he suggested that this term is no longer adequate. These individuals and groups may be even more sensitive to status than are states, he noted, because they may have few other assets. He identified this as a very promising line of research.

Lynn-Jones also agreed with Goldgeier on the importance of interdisciplinary research and the sharing of conceptual thinking across fields, noting that such approaches are particularly important for dealing with general questions of cybersecurity, Internet governance, and information warfare. However, he cautioned that interdisciplinary efforts are not always successful. In his view, the most promising approach is to compel a group of individual researchers from different disciplines to collaborate in addressing a defined problem.

Thompson offered a few additional thoughts about status, noting that it was a prevalent research topic in the 1960s and 1970s but thereafter received much less attention. He suggested that it is valuable to study this topic now in part because it reflects a reaction to structural changes taking place in the international system. However, he cautioned that it is not a "generic entity" and that the status concerns of different states vary. "Some Russians want to go back to the USSR; some Chinese currently want regional hegemony . . . and what the Iranians want is neither of those," he noted. He suggested that questions of status need to be interpreted within their contexts.

Thompson also urged caution in analysis of cyberwarfare. In his view, little is really known about the extent of cyberconflict, "who does it, and when." He believes systematic analysis of the flow and structure of cyberconflict, if only for a sample period, is badly needed to support analysis.

Thompson closed with an argument for taking a very long view of history in thinking about trends and predictions. While he acknowledged that the parameters certainly change over time, he asserted that "when you get the same outcomes repeated millennia after millennia, it is more possible to make that kind of a prediction. In some cases, long-term history can be used to make forecasts."

Appendix A

Statement of Task for the Decadal Survey of Social and Behavioral Sciences for Applications to National Security

The National Academies of Sciences, Engineering, and Medicine will carry out a decadal survey on the social and behavioral sciences (SBS) in areas relevant to national security in two integrated phases. The first phase, a national summit (workshop), was completed in fall 2016. The statement of task for the second phase, a consensus process, is below.

An ad hoc consensus committee, drawing on membership from the summit steering committee, will be appointed to conduct the decadal survey aimed at identifying opportunities that are poised to contribute significantly to the Intelligence Community's (IC's) analytic responsibilities. The study will identify opportunities throughout the social sciences (e.g., sociology, demography, political science, economics, and anthropology) and from behavioral sciences (e.g., psychology, cognition, and neuroscience) and will draw on discussions at the summit to frame its inquiry. Attention will also be paid to work in allied professional disciplines, such as engineering, business, and law, and a full variety of cross-disciplinary, historical, case study, participant, and phronetic approaches.

The committee will work with the Office of the Director of National Intelligence (ODNI) and security community members to understand government needs and expectations. The final report will be based on the committee's consideration of broad national security priorities; relevant capabilities of elements within the security community to support and apply SBS research findings; cost and technical readiness; likely growth of research programs; emerging SBS data, procedures, personnel, and other resources; and opportunities to leverage related research activities not directly supported by government. The committee will specify a range of relevant work that could be useful to the IC for their consideration in developing future research priorities.

The committee's primary tasks will be to:

1. Assess progress in addressing selected major social and behavioral scientific challenges that might prove useful to national security. Include discussion of approaches that are gaining strength and those that are losing strength.
2. Identify SBS opportunities that can be used to guide security community investment decisions and application efforts over the next 10 years.
3. Specify approaches to facilitate productive interchange between the security community and the external social science research community.
4. Reflect on the application of the decadal model to the SBS and identify lessons learned (insights into how to approach and perform the decadal survey process) and promising practices (activities that could facilitate future decadal surveys in the SBS and similar disciplines and maximize their ultimate utilities to sponsors and the scientific community).

Appendix B

Workshop Agenda

EMERGING TRENDS AND METHODS IN INTERNATIONAL SECURITY

October 11, 2017

Keck Center
500 Fifth Street, NW
Washington, DC
Room 208

8:30 a.m.	**Workshop Registration Opens**
9:00 a.m.	**Workshops Commence**

9:00 a.m.	**WELCOME AND OVERVIEW OF MEETING**
	Sujeeta Bhatt, Study Director
	    Audience information
	Paul Sackett, University of Minnesota, SBS Decadal Survey Chair
	    Welcome
	David Honey, Director of Science and Technology, ODNI, Study Sponsor
	    Sponsor perspective and context for study and workshops

9:30 a.m.	**Opening Remarks on the Emerging Trends and Methods in International Security** *Jeffrey Taliaferro,* Tufts University; SBS Decadal Survey Committee Member; Workshop Steering Committee Member

Research Panel Presentations and Discussion

9:40 a.m.   **Panel 1: Reputation, Power, and Status**

This panel will consider the international security implications and changing nature of power, legitimacy, and status in the international system.

Jeffrey Taliaferro, Session Moderator

Steven Ward, Cornell University
    Status and International Security
Deborah Larson, University of California, Los Angeles
    Shifting Power and the Legitimacy of the International Pecking Order
Amanda Murdie, University of Georgia
    Beyond States: Measuring Reputation, Power, and Status in Nonstate Actors

10:25 a.m.   **Response to Presentations**
Suzanne Fry, National Intelligence Council

10:35 a.m.   **Moderated Open Discussion**

11:05 a.m.   **Panel 2: Strategic Use of Information**

This panel will examine topics related to cyber policy and security. Speakers will address issues such as Internet regulation and control in authoritarian governments, cyber espionage, and the manipulation of information as a component of hybrid warfare.

Sumit Ganguly, Indiana University; Session Moderator; Workshop Steering Committee Member

Herb Lin, Stanford University
    On Cyber-Enabled Information Warfare and Influence Operations
Jacklyn Kerr, Stanford University
    Authoritarian Soft Power? Internet Content, Information Conflict, and the Future of Free Expression

	Richard J. Harknett, University of Cincinnati *Cyber Persistence: Rethinking Security and Seizing the Strategic Cyber Initiative*
11:50 a.m.	**Response to Presentations** *Suzanne Fry*, National Intelligence Council
12:00 p.m.	**Moderated Open Discussion**
12:30 p.m.	**LUNCH**

1:30 p.m.	**Panel 3: Forecasting Methods and Topics**
	
	This panel will explore the international security implications and methods of forecasting democratic backsliding, military conflict and violence, epidemics, and environmental security.
	
	Sumit Ganguly, Session Moderator
	
	Kacey Ernst, Arizona University
	    From Prediction to Practice: Integrating Forecasting Models Into Public Health Education and Response
	Afreen Siddiqi, Massachusetts Institute of Technology
	    Formulating Expectations for Future Water Availability in Arid Regions
	Jennifer Dresden, Georgetown University
	    Authoritarian Backsliding: Drivers, Trends, and Implications
	Christopher Gelpi, Ohio State University
	    Connecting Theory to Policy with Forecasting

2:30 p.m.	**Response to Presentations** *Suzanne Fry*, National Intelligence Council
2:40 p.m.	**Moderated Open Discussion**
3:10 p.m.	**BREAK**

3:25 p.m.	**Methodology** *Andrew Bennett*, Georgetown University; Workshop Steering Committee Member
3:45 p.m.	**Panel 4: Discussant Panel** *This panel will reflect on and discuss the morning and afternoon topic panels.* *Andrew Bennett*, Session Moderator *James Goldgeier*, American University *Sean Lynn-Jones*, Harvard University *William R. Thompson*, Indiana University
4:45 p.m.	**Closing Remarks** *Jeffrey Taliaferro*, Tufts University
5:00 p.m.	**ADJOURN**

Appendix C

Participants List

Listed here are the individuals who attended one or more of three workshops held October 11, 2017, to gather information for the Decadal Survey of Social and Behavioral Sciences for Applications to National Security.

Vincent Alcazar
Vincent Alcazar, LLC

Alexandra Beatty
National Academies

Andrew Bennett
Georgetown University

Gary G. Berntson
Ohio State University

Sujeeta Bhatt
National Academies

Jordan A. Blenner
Lewis-Burke Associates, LLC

Matthew Brashears
University of South Carolina

Christa Brelsford
Oak Ridge National Laboratory

David Broniatowski
George Washington University

Dennis Buede
Innovative Decisions, Inc.

Rita Bush
National Security Agency

Kathleen Carley
Carnegie Mellon University

Lina Cepeda
United Nations

Guido Cervone
Pennsylvania State University

Hsinchun Chen
University of Arizona

Richard Cincotta
Stimson Center

Kyle Clark
U.S. Department of Homeland Security

Noshir Contractor
Northwestern University

Bradley Cooke
National Science Foundation

Chris Cox
Defense Intelligence Agency

Thelma Cox
National Academies

Skyler Cranmer
Ohio State University

Bruce Crawford
Independent Researcher

Leslie DeChurch
Northwestern University

Daniel Demus
Defense Threat Reduction Agency

David Dornisch
U.S. Government Accountability Office

Barbara Anne Dosher
University of California, Irvine

Jennifer Dresden
Georgetown University

William Dressler
University of Alabama

Anna Duran
Avatar Research Institute

Jesse A. Egbert
Northern Arizona University

Kacey Ernst
Arizona University

Emily Falk
University of Pennsylvania

Scott Feld
Purdue University

Suzanne Fry
National Intelligence Council

George G.
U.S. Government

Sumit Ganguly
Indiana University

Michele Gelfand
University of Maryland

Christopher Gelpi
The Ohio State University

James Goldgeier
American University

APPENDIX C

Benjamin Golub
Harvard University

Hal Greenwald
MITRE

Winston Harris
Defense Threat Reduction Agency

Richard Harknett
University of Cincinnati

Jesse Hoey
University of Waterloo

Michael Holtje
U.S. Department of Treasury

David Honey
Office of the Director of National Intelligence

John Hoven
Independent Consultant

Judith Jacobson
Innovative Decisions, Inc.

Gary Jin
U.S. Department of Homeland Security

Jeffrey C. Johnson
University of Florida

Kenneth Joseph
Northeastern University

Regina Joseph
New York University

Dan Kahan
Yale University

Sallie Keller
Virginia Polytechnic Institute and State University

Jacklyn Kerr
Stanford University

Giuseppe (Joe) Labianca
University of Kentucky

Deborah Larson
University of California, Los Angeles

Mark Liberman
University of Pennsylvania

Herb Lin
Stanford University

Sean Lynn-Jones
Harvard University

Anthony Mann
National Academies

David Matsumoto
San Francisco State University

Shana McLean
IARPA

Carmen Medina
MedinAnalytics, LLC

Asma Melebrai
Government Contractor

Katherine Meyer
National Science Foundation

Marc Dean Millot
Good Harbor Partners

Mahmoud Moamenah
Government Contractor

Markus Mobius
Microsoft Research

Fran P. Moore
FPM Consulting, LLC

Amanda Murdie
University of Georgia

Dhiraj Murthy
University of Texas

Kent Myers
Office of the Director of National Intelligence

Zachary Neal
Michigan State University

Howard C. Nusbaum
National Science Foundation

Robert O'Connor
National Science Foundation

Nedim Ogelman
U.S. Department of State

Carolyn Parkinson
University of California, Los Angeles

Randolph H. Pherson
Pherson Associates, LLC

Jennarose Placitella
University of Pennsylvania

Ted Plasse
U.S. Department of Defense

Alyson Reed
Linguistic Society of America

Philip Resnik
University of Maryland

Joy Rohde
University of Michigan

Benjamin Ryan
Gallup, Inc.

Paul R. Sackett
University of Minnesota

Laura Sappelsa
ANSER

Julie Schuck
National Academies

Afreen Siddiqi
Massachusetts Institute of Technology

Michael Siri
National Academies

Robert Smith
University of Maryland

Laura Steckman
MITRE

Anita Street
Office of the Director of National Intelligence

Jim Sullivan
Central Intelligence Agency

Gwyneth Sutherlin
Geographic Services, Inc.

Jeffrey Taliaferro
Tufts University

Steve Thompson
Office of the Director of National Intelligence

William R. Thompson
Indiana University

Elizabeth Townsend
National Academies

Lisa Troyer
Army Research Office

Garrett Tyson
National Academies

Stuart Umpleby
George Washington University

Alexander Volfovsky
Duke University

Kate Von Holle
University of Chicago

Barbara Wanchisen
National Academies

Steven Ward
Cornell University

Susan Weller
University of Texas

Mitzi Wertheim
Naval Postgraduate School

Renée L. Wilson Gaines
National Academies

Jeremy Wolfe
Brigham & Women's Hospital, Harvard Medical School

Mary Zalesny
Defense Threat Reduction Agency

Appendix D

Biographical Sketches of Steering Committee Members and Presenters

Andrew Bennett (*Committee Member*) is professor of government at Georgetown University. He is the cofounder, together with Colin Elman and David Collier, of the Institute for Qualitative and Multimethod Research, which teaches research methods to 200 Ph.D. students each June at Syracuse University. He was the first president of the American Political Science Association section on qualitative methods, and he has taught case study methods to graduate students in a number of countries abroad as well as the United States. He has served as a consultant on case study research projects for The World Bank, the U.S. Department of Defense, and the U.S. Intelligence Community. Dr. Bennett earned a B.A. in political science from Stanford University and an M.P.P. and a Ph.D. in public policy from the Kennedy School of Government at Harvard University.

Sujeeta Bhatt (*Study Director*) is a senior program officer with the National Academies of Sciences, Engineering, and Medicine and study director for the Decadal Survey of Social and Behavioral Sciences and Applications to National Security. She was formerly a research scientist at the Defense Intelligence Agency (DIA) and was detailed to the Federal Bureau of Investigation's High-Value Detainee Interrogation Group (HIG). Prior to that, she was an assistant professor in the Department of Radiology at the Georgetown University Medical Center on detail to DIA/HIG. Her work at DIA and HIG entailed identifying knowledge gaps and developing and managing research projects to address those gaps. Her work in the Intelligence Community focused on the psychological and neuroscience bases for credibility assessment, biometrics, insider threat, intelligence interviewing and interrogation methods, and the development of research-to-practice modules on interrogation-related topics to promote the use of evidence-based practice in interviews/interrogations. Dr. Bhatt holds a Ph.D. in behavioral neuroscience from American University.

Jennifer Raymond Dresden (*Presenter*) is assistant teaching professor and associate director of the Democracy and Governance Program at Georgetown University. Her research lies at the intersection of comparative politics and international relations, with particular emphasis on the political outcomes of civil wars. Her book project combines quantitative and qualitative methods and draws on field research conducted in Sierra Leone and Mozambique. She previously taught at the George Washington University. She regularly serves as a training facilitator for the U.S. Department of State and has contributed to case study research for the Political Instability Task Force. She holds an A.B. in government from Harvard University, an M.Litt. in peace and conflict studies from the University of St. Andrews, and a Ph.D. in government from Georgetown University.

Kacey Ernst (*Presenter*) is associate professor and program director of undergraduate programs at the Mel and Enid Zuckerman College of Public Health, University of Arizona. Her work examines the role of weather, climate, and climate change in the emergence of infectious diseases, specifically vectorborne diseases, including malaria, Zika, and dengue. She works within a highly interdisciplinary team of climatologists, anthropologists, entomologists, and geographers to develop models that predict both the seasonal and the long-term trends of *Aedes*-borne viruses. In addition to developing a better understanding of how vectorborne disease risk may change in the future, she seeks to engage communities in developing capacity-building and resilience strategies to reduce their risk. She has conducted fieldwork in Ghana, Kenya, Indonesia, Mexico, and Jamaica to better understand the current and future response capacity of predominantly rural populations. In the past 2 years, she has led a team of scientist and public health stakeholders in developing Kidenga, a mobile community-based surveillance application and educational tool to enhance the detection and awareness of vectorborne disease transmission. She holds a B.A. in chemistry and biology from Lawrence University and an M.P.H. and Ph.D. in epidemiology from the University of Michigan.

Suzanne Fry (*Presenter*) is director of the Strategic Futures Group at the National Intelligence Council (NIC). The NIC supports the director of national intelligence in his role as head of the Intelligence Community and serves as a bridge between the intelligence and policy communities. At the NIC, Dr. Fry is responsible for global issues and long-range analysis, as well as the *Global Trends* series, the NIC's flagship unclassified assessment of the future strategic landscape. Prior to joining the NIC, she worked on a range of governance, instability, and strategic warning issues worldwide and led the U.S. Intelligence Community's Political Instability Task Force. She earned a B.A. in government and international studies from the University of Notre Dame and a Ph.D. in politics from New York University.

Sumit Ganguly (*Committee Member*) is a professor of political science, holds the Rabindranath Tagore chair in Indian cultures and civilizations, and directs the Center on American and Global Security at Indiana University, Bloomington. A specialist in the international and comparative politics of South Asia, he previously taught at James Madison College of Michigan State University, Hunter College of the City University of New York, the School of Public and International Affairs at Columbia University, and the University of Texas at Austin, as well as at Northwestern University, where he was visiting Buffet professor of international studies. He has also been a fellow/guest scholar at the Woodrow Wilson International Center for Scholars; the Center on International Security and Cooperation; the Center on Democracy, Development, and the Rule of Law at Stanford University; and the Institute of Defense Studies and Analysis in New Delhi. In 2017–2018, he will be a visiting fellow at the Strategic Studies Institute of the U.S. Army War College. Dr. Ganguly received a B.A. in English and political science from Berea College, an M.A. in political science from Miami University, and a Ph.D. in political science from the University of Illinois at Urbana–Champaign.

Christopher Gelpi (*Presenter*) is chair of peace studies and conflict resolution at the Mershon Center for International Security and professor of political science at the Ohio State University. His primary research interests are the sources of international militarized conflict and strategies for international conflict resolution. He is currently engaged in research on American public opinion and the use of military force and on statistical models for forecasting military conflict and transnational terrorist violence. His work has also encompassed American civil–military relations and the use of force, the impact of democracy and trade on international conflict, the role of norms in crisis bargaining, alliances as instruments of control, diversionary wars, deterrence theory, and the influence of the international system on the outbreak of violence. He received an A.B. in political science from Stanford University and a Ph.D. in political science from the University of Michigan.

James Goldgeier (*Presenter*) is visiting senior fellow at the Council on Foreign Relations. He is also professor of international relations and served as dean of the School of International Service at American University from 2011–2017. Previously, he was a professor of political science and international affairs at the George Washington University. He also taught at Cornell University and has held a number of public policy appointments. In addition, he has held appointments at the Woodrow Wilson International Center for Scholars, the Brookings Institution, and the Center for International Security and Cooperation. From 2001 to 2005, he directed the George Washington University's Institute for European, Russian, and Eurasian Studies. He is the recipient of the Edgar S. Furniss book award in national and international security and co-recipient of the Georgetown University Lepgold book prize in international relations. He received an A.B. in government from Harvard University and an M.A. and Ph.D. in political science from the University of California.

Richard J. Harknett (*Presenter*) is professor and head of the Department of Political Science at the University of Cincinnati (UC). He served in 2017 as the inaugural U.S.–UK Fulbright scholar in cybersecurity, University of Oxford, United Kingdom, and in 2016 as the first scholar-in-residence at the U.S. Cyber Command and National Security Agency. He has provided invited lectures internationally and numerous presentations and briefings to government agencies and congressional offices on Capitol Hill. He has testified on cybersecurity to the Ohio State Legislature and served as the governor's appointee on the State of Ohio's Cybersecurity, Education, and Economic Development Council while contributing to the writing of Ohio's cybersecurity strategy. He has been Fulbright professor of international relations at the Diplomatic Academy, Vienna, Austria, where he continues to hold a professorial lectureship; Boyd-Lubker visiting scholar at Western Kentucky University; and Edith C. Alexander distinguished teaching professor and distinguished service professor at McMicken College, UC. He has been honored with faculty awards and served as chair of the University Faculty and chair of the Charles Phelps Taft Research Center at UC. He earned a B.A. from Villanova University and his Ph.D. from the Johns Hopkins University.

David A. Honey (*Sponsor*) serves as director of science and technology and as assistant deputy director of national intelligence for science and technology in the Office of the Director of National Intelligence. He is responsible for the development of effective strategies, policies, and programs that lead to the successful integration of science and technology capabilities into operational systems. Prior to this assignment, he served as deputy assistant secretary of defense, research, in the Office of the Assistant Secretary of Defense. He was director of the Defense Advanced Research Projects Agency's Strategic Technology Office, director of the Advanced Technology Office, and deputy director and program manager of the Microsystems Technology Office. He is a retired Air Force lieutenant colonel who began his military career as a pilot. He received a Ph.D. in solid state science from Syracuse University.

Judith Kelley (*Committee Member*) is Terry Sanford professor of public policy, professor of political science, and senior associate dean at the Duke Sanford School of Public Policy. She is also a senior fellow with the Kenan Institute for Ethics. In 2009–2010, she was a visiting fellow at the University of Aarhus, Denmark. Her research interests focus on the role of international actors in promoting political and human rights reforms. Her work also focuses on how states, international organizations, and nongovernmental organizations can promote domestic political reforms in problem states and how international norms, laws, and other governance tools influence state behavior. Substantively, her work addresses human rights and democracy, international election observation, and human trafficking. Her past work has focused on the International Criminal Court, the European Union, and other international organizations. In 2012, she was inducted into the Bass Society of Fellows at Duke, which recognizes faculty for excellence in both teaching and scholarship. The Smith Richardson Foundation has supported her as a policy and strategy fellow. She received her Ph.D. in public policy from Harvard University.

Jacklyn Kerr (*Presenter*) is a postdoctoral research fellow at the Center for Global Security Research, Lawrence Livermore National Laboratory. Her research examines cybersecurity and information security strategy, Internet governance, and the Internet policies of nondemocratic regimes. Dr. Kerr was a 2015–2016 science, technology, and public policy predoctoral fellow with the Cyber Security Project at the Belfer Center for Science and International Affairs. She was also a visiting scholar at the Davis Center for Russian and Eurasian Studies at Harvard University and a cybersecurity predoctoral fellow at Stanford University's Center for International Security and Cooperation in 2014–2015. She has held research fellowships in Russia, Kazakhstan, and Qatar and has previous professional experience as a software engineer. She holds a B.A.S. in mathematics and Slavic languages and literatures and an M.A. in Russian, East European, and Eurasian studies from Stanford University, and an M.A. and Ph.D. in government from Georgetown University.

Deborah Welch Larson (*Presenter*) is professor of political science at the University of California, Los Angeles (UCLA). She draws on historical, psychological, and political evidence to understand foreign policy decision making. Her professorship in the department is supported by the International Studies and Overseas Programs administration at UCLA. Dr. Larson has studied the development of Cold War belief systems by researching postwar U.S. policy makers from a cognitive psychological perspective. She has also studied game theory, exchange theory, and bargaining theory to explain how mistrust prevented the United States and the Soviet Union from reaching agreements in the early Cold War. She is currently developing a framework for evaluating the quality of political judgments in the profoundly uncertain international environment. She received her Ph.D. in political science from Stanford University.

Herb Lin (*Presenter*) is senior research scholar for cyber policy and security at the Center for International Security and Cooperation and Hank J. Holland fellow in cyber policy and security at the Hoover Institution, both at Stanford University. His research interests relate broadly to policy-related dimensions of cybersecurity and cyberspace, and particularly the use of offensive operations in cyberspace as instruments of national policy. In addition to his positions at Stanford University, he is chief scientist (emeritus) for the Computer Science and Telecommunications Board of the National Academies of Sciences, Engineering, and Medicine; adjunct senior research scholar and senior fellow in cybersecurity (not in residence) at the Saltzman Institute for War and Peace Studies in the School for International and Public Affairs, Columbia University; and a member of the Science and Security Board of the *Bulletin of the Atomic Scientists*. He recently served on President Obama's Commission on Enhancing National Cybersecurity. Previously, he was a professional staff member and staff scientist for the House Armed Services Committee (1986–1990), where his portfolio included defense policy and arms control issues. He received his Ph.D. in physics from the Massachusetts Institute of Technology.

Sean Lynn-Jones (*Presenter*) is editor of *International Security*, a quarterly journal based at Harvard's Belfer Center for Science and International Affairs. He is also series editor of the *Belfer Center Studies in International Security*, a book series published by MIT Press. He previously served as managing editor of *International Security* (1987–1991). He is a member of the board of the International Security and Arms Control Section of the American Political Science Association. His research interests include international relations theory, U.S. foreign policy, and why rivalries end peacefully.

Amanda Murdie (*Presenter*) is Dean Rusk scholar of international relations and professor of international affairs in the School of Public and International Affairs, University of Georgia. She is also director of graduate studies for the Department of International Affairs. In 2015, she served as president of the International Studies Association-Midwest. Along with Cooper Drury, she was 2016 program chair for the International Studies Association Annual Convention. She studies international relations, specializing in the behavior of international nongovernmental organizations (INGOs) and their interactions with states, local populations, and intergovernmental organizations. She is also interested in human rights/security, dissent, development, quantitative methodologies, formal modeling, and conflict more generally. She has worked with both the policy and the nongovernmental organization communities to develop new quantitative measures that capture the power of human security INGOs and track the spread of human security norms among nonstate actors. She received a B.S. and an M.A. in political science from Kansas State University and a Ph.D. in political science from Emory University.

Paul Sackett (*Decadal Survey Chair*) is Beverly and Richard Fink distinguished professor of psychology and liberal arts at the University of Minnesota. His research interests revolve around various aspects of testing and assessment in workplace, educational, and military settings. He has served as president of the Society for Industrial and Organizational Psychology, as cochair of the committee producing the Standards for Educational and Psychological Testing, as a member of the National Research Council's Board on Testing and Assessment, as chair of the American Psychological Association's (APA's) Committee on Psychological Tests and Assessments, and as chair of APA's Board of Scientific Affairs. He holds a Ph.D. in industrial/organizational psychology from the Ohio State University.

Afreen Siddiqi (*Presenter*) is a visiting scholar with the Science, Technology, and Public Policy Program at Harvard Kennedy School's Belfer Center for Science and International Affairs. She is also a research scientist at the Massachusetts Institute of Technology (MIT) and an associate director of the MIT Strategic Engineering Research Group. Her research expertise is at the intersection of technology, policy, and international development. She combines quantitative tools and qualitative methods for analysis of complex sociotechnical systems. In recent work she has analyzed critical linkages among water, energy, and food systems in the Middle East and Pakistan; emerging trends in scientific research in the Middle East and North Africa; and methods for systems architecture and design trade space analysis. She has been a recipient of the Amelia Earhart fellowship, the Richard D. DuPont fellowship, and the Rene H. Miller prize in systems engineering. Her work experience encompasses positions in engineering, consulting, and teaching. She holds an S.B. in mechanical engineering and an S.M. and a Ph.D. in aerospace systems from MIT.

Jeffrey W. Taliaferro (*Committee Member*) is an associate professor of political science at Tufts University. His research and teaching focus on security studies, international relations theory, international history and politics, U.S. foreign policy, intelligence, and national security. He is currently a fellow at the Woodrow Wilson International Center for Scholars, where he is completing work on the politics of alliance coercion and nuclear nonproliferation in U.S. foreign policy during the second half of the Cold War. He has been a member of the Director of the Central Intelligence Agency's Historical Review Panel since 2008. He earned a bachelor's degree in history and political science from Duke University and a Ph.D. in government from Harvard University.

William R. Thompson (*Presenter*) is distinguished professor emeritus and Rogers chair of political science emeritus at Indiana University. He is a past president of the International Studies Association. He began his career studying military coups and conducted research that showed that coups are often contagious and spread from one country to another. He uses quantitative research methods to study long-term patterns of change in the global system. His research has focused particularly on theories about the importance of technological change and the rise of new industries as a major factor in politics. He received a B.A. in economics and political science and an M.A. and a Ph.D. in political science from the University of Washington.

Gregory F. Treverton (*Committee Chair*) is professor of the practice of international relations at the University of Southern California. He was chairman of the National Intelligence Council from 2014–2017. Previously, he directed the RAND Corporation's Center for Global Risk and Security, and before that its Intelligence Policy Center and its International Security and Defense Policy Center; he was also associate dean of the Pardee RAND Graduate School. He has served in government for the first Senate Select Committee on Intelligence; handled Europe for the National Security Council; and served as vice chair of the National Intelligence Council, overseeing the writing of America's National Intelligence Estimates. He has taught at Harvard and Columbia universities, and he has been a senior fellow at the Council on Foreign Relations and deputy director of the International Institute for Strategic Studies in London. He holds a B.A. summa cum laude from Princeton University and an M.P.P and a Ph.D. in economics and politics from Harvard.

Steven Ward (*Presenter*) is an assistant professor of government at Cornell University and a Carnegie junior faculty fellow at Stanford University's Center for International Security and Cooperation. His current research focuses on analyzing the influence of status ambitions and anxiety on domestic politics and foreign policy. His work has addressed how status concerns can push rising states to launch costly, risky challenges to the international status quo, and tested this account against the records of Wilhelmine Germany, Imperial Japan, Nazi Germany, and the United States around the turn of the 20th century. He holds a Ph.D. from Georgetown University.